S0-CCI-357

Kavet's **internet sites**

for **Men** Over **50** 50 50 50

PUBLISHED BY
BOSTON AMERICA CORP.

www.bostonamerica.com

125 WALNUT STREET, WATERTOWN, MASSACHUSETTS 02472

TEL: (617) 923 1111 • FAX: (617) 923 8839

KAVET'S INTERNET SITES FOR MEN OVER 50: ISBN 1-889647-56-X. PRINTED IN U.S.A.

Written by Herbert I. Kavet
Edited by Karen C. Kavet
Designed by Victoria Bocash of *Inktree Design*

Table of Contents

table of contents

Introduction

Fifty is half a century. That's serious years and if you're like me you need all the help you can get. That's what this book is about. Internet sites to help 50 year olds. We need help with stomachs and hair and memory and driving at night; with financing kid's college and understanding what they're saying. This book has everything we 50 year olds need to know, listed and categorized and it even has an index to help you find everything unless I forgot that page. I forget a lot these days so please excuse any lapses in this book.

Perhaps the most valuable part of this book is not so much the specific sites listed but the knowledge that sites exist on these subjects. Once you realize there are places you can get information on Viagra or snoring or beer or fly fishing or exotic vacations you'll have little trouble finding more sites yourself.

Apology & Disclaimer

When I wrote this book all the sites listed were live and available. When you go to some of them, you'll find they've disappeared. God only knows where they go. Some will disappear and some will come back an hour later and some will somehow evolve into a site for Korean folk remedies translated into Hungarian. The internet is indeed a mysterious place. My best advice, if this happens, is to simply move on to the next site. There are plenty listed in each category and the ones that are anxious to sell you something will probably be available longer than some loony trying to cure indigestion with grass seeds or teenager's homesite.

Lots of people are trying to get rich using the internet, me included, and many of the sites listed here are commercial enterprises trying to suck you into $29.95 a month. If these people are successful I suppose their sites will be around for a long while. I've tried to find mostly free sites but these also tend to disappear when the host gets bored with working for nothing. Regardless, while you can find all these sites for yourself (especially if your time is worth 9 cents an hour) I've done lots of the leg work and locating just one or two useful sites will be easily worth more than the ridiculously low price of this book.

That said, the author, publisher and distributors of this book cannot take responsibility for what you find or don't find or what these sites lead you to, even the pornographic stuff that I didn't intend, or what you may buy and then get stuck with or any of the fascinating, frustrating and endless paths of the internet. Hey, it's the internet. What do you want me to do.

How to Use Your Computer

In case you got a new computer along with this book you may need some instruction on how to use it. Actually, my wife taught me. If you have kids get one of them to hook it up and teach you how to get online. If you never bothered to have kids don't worry. First of all everyone has some geek friend who knows all about computers and will be thrilled if you ask them to help. Let these people set up everything so all you have to do is push a button or two and click on a little icon and the information pops up. Whatever you do don't open the instructions that came with the computer or use the HELP menu and try to do it yourself. Not only will this frustrate you but it also voids your warranty.

Once you get online have your friend show you where all the pornographic sites are – no I'm kidding – ask him where the little box is where you type in the www stuff. Then type in the line of gibberish and a notice will appear that this site can't be found. There will be a bunch of suggestions on what to do but none of them will work so just go on to another site.

Getting Started

 www.realage.com

> Real age lets you fill in a profile and it will calculate your true age. Actually it sounds like you're applying for life insurance and maybe you are.
>
> Once you find out how old you really are, and if indeed you are 50, you can check into:

 www.50something.net

> Can you believe a site just for us 50 year olds? Perhaps a little simplistic but it's nice to know someone is thinking about us.
>
> If you've found that you are not around 50 years old you'd better try to get your money back on this book but if I have anything to say about it you won't be successful.

Before you begin you'd better make sure you are really 50 years old. Here is a site that gives your real age rather than that silly chronological age your parents gave you. Maybe you feel 65 years old when you get up in the morning but later when you see an attractive young lady at the office you have the behavior of a 19 year old and then when faced with a double chocolate fudge ice cream cone you drop to 9. How old are you anyway?

Men's Health

You know the old saying, "If you have your health you have everything." You start believing this when you're 50 and your back goes out or you get winded on a flight of stairs or you start swallowing antacid pills like M&M's. This section gives you information on your aging body and some ideas for keeping it young. They do work. I may be 50 but I have the body of a 49 year old.

General Men's Health

www.aomc.org/HOD2/general/menshealth.html

The Arnot Ogden Medical Center site for Men's Health and Wellness. Information on all sort of men's problems from hair loss to prostate to jock itch. Super information even if it does scare you to death.

www.healthtouch.com

An index of male health problems. A well written non technical review of the major diseases that are out to get us. Just type in the disease or health category that you'd like to lose sleep over and a bunch of articles come up.

www.intelihealth.com

This is Johns Hopkins home site of medical information and there is so much here that if you read it all you will probably qualify to practice medicine. It tells what everything is, how to treat it and best of all when to call your doctor.

www.malehealthcenter.com

Another great site for all you hypochondriacs out there. It is run by the Men's Health Center in Dallas. Scroll down and see all the things that can go wrong with you.

medic.med.uth.tmc.edu/ptnt/00000391.htm

Information about exercising for your heart, fats and cholesterol, prostate, and cancer screening. You can search for much more if you have the courage.

www.healthwatchers.com/hw/default.asp

Mostly they are trying to sell you various potions that cure everything but it's kind of fun.

Okay, we're not invincible any more. We go for an annual physical and watch our diet. We can't bend over quite like we used to. We're sore for 3 days after playing something with 30 year olds that we shouldn't be playing. We find our stomachs are suddenly very choosy about what they will accept, imagine that just maybe our hair is thinning, and have a back that "goes out" more than we do. It's time to start learning something about what makes our bodies tick and what we can expect from them. These sites will do that.

General men's health

One thing that I started doing once I reached 50 was to read and believe every article on health that I came across. "Broccoli Prevents Cancer", I eat it raw twice a day; "Salt Causes Hypertension", there go the potato chips; "Carrots Improve Night Vision" I turn into a rabbit. This leads to problems, of course, when one article extols coffee and the next damns it, but I've decided to just go with the latest postmark. The sites listed here give, I hope, the latest "skinny".

www.drkoop.com

Former Surgeon General Dr. C. E. Koop heads this site with an enormous amount of free information on thousands of medical questions.

www.onhealth.com/ch1/index.asp

Just type in a problem or condition and you'll be buried with information.

www.healthandage.com/fpatient.htm

If you want to see where you'll be in 10 years visit this site. Actually I don't recommend it. Alzheimer's, depression, incontinence; it's all pretty scary.

www.mediconsult.com

The latest information on men's health in an easy chatty format.

www.healthanswers.com

This is one hell of a medical library. Just type in the part you are interested in and let them terrify you with what can go wrong with it.

www.healthy.net/menshealth

A load of information from a list of every medical school to reports on every disease from several sources to articles on andropause which is a controversial counterpart to women's menopause.

Medical Sites

•••⋮ **www.healthfinder.gov**

This site leads to lots of reliable medical sites, It's run by your government and they wouldn't do anything to mislead you.

•••⋮ **www.nih.gov/health**

The National Institute of Health with direct links to the specific institute that supports research related to your health concern.

•••⋮ **www.mayo.edu**

The famous Mayo Clinic hosts this site and visiting it is a lot better than traveling to Minnesota in February.

•••⋮ **www.medscape.com**

A very comprehensive collection of authoritative medical information and education. It may be geared to doctors but by 50 you're probably smart enough to understand it.

•••⋮ **www.americanheart.org**

The American Heart Association keeps you informed about your heart as well as nicely asking you for a donation.

•••⋮ **www.cancer.org**

The American Cancer Society will bring you up to date on all the latest preventive measures you can take.

I don't want you guys to think I'm a hypochondriac or anything but these are great medical sites that will explain everything the doctor is too busy to explain. If you'd like your doctor to spend more than 2 minutes explaining things, you're going to have to increase your health plan cost by 40%.

Hair Loss and Growth

Until recently there was little other than sticking a rug on your head to handle the balding problem. Then Rogaine came out and was legitimatized by your needing a prescription to get it, and hair regeneration became a serious field. These sites will expose you to lots of options from pills that may really work, to weaving in hair, to stuff you spray to make your scalp black.

www.regrowth.com

A very comprehensive site with all sorts of treatments and remedies from green tea to transplants and an honest evaluation of each.

hometown.aol.com/hairbook/index.htm

Hair Loss Information Center gives a superb background on hair and its characteristics and a detailed analysis of each kind of treatment.

www.propecia.com

Details on Propecia, a prescription drug from Merck which has been found helpful in controlling baldness.

www.hairsource.com

This site sells all sorts of non prescription hair loss remedies of a kind that used to be recommended by your bald barber. Read the above sites before spending money.

www.unibio.com

This site sells Natural Cosmeceutuals (whatever that is) and promises amazing hair growth from some pretty expensive stuff. Again, read the first 2 sites first.

Hair Loss and Growth

www.prothik.com

Pro Thik is an aerosol hair thickening system. It looks like you spray this stuff on and it either colors your scalp to look like hair or sticks to what you have to make it look like more.

www.ahlc.org

The American Hair Loss Council's non profit site that facilitates the exchange of information about hair loss. Loads of sound information.

www.pslgroup.com/HAIRLOSS.HTM

Doctors' guide to hair loss. A good discussion.

www.morehair.com

A great deal of very sound information. I wish I had time to read it all because I'm getting a little thin on top.

www.regenhair.com

A lot of promises that go against all the above medically approved advice, but even quacks have to earn a living.

www.luxor-of-paris.com/prices.htm

Another herbal remedy "guaranteed" to prevent baldness. From Paris no less.

Some of the non commercial hair loss sites not only give you information on legitimate possible cures but also details on what various shampoos and hair colorings do to your hair. There are a bunch of others that promise re-growth with various concoctions that would be very funny if they didn't cost a lot of money.

Men's Health Magazines

A good health magazine will keep you up-to-date on the latest theories about what you should and shouldn't do so you do and don't do those things until the next monthly issue when they change their minds. Coffee, aspirin, margarine, vitamin C, garlic, fiber, whatever. If you wait a month or two it'll change.

www.menshealth.com

Fitness, sex health and sports at the home site of Men's Health Magazine.

www.vitality.com/vfm.html

Vitality Magazine's site with a fair list of tips on health.

www.newsdirectory.com/news/magazine/health

A directory of about 35 health magazines from the U. S. and U.K., many on specialized subjects like massage and deafness.

www.mensfitness.com

Another good fitness magazine covering training, nutrition, health and gear and probably sex since they all cover sex.

bewell.healthgate.com/menshealth/index.asp

An online men's magazine that has new interesting articles each week.

Medical Concerns - Prostate

comed.com/Prostate

An extensive prostate cancer information link with information on everything from risks to diagnosis to help and support.

www.gretmar.com/webdoctor/bph.html

A substantial article on prostate enlargement known as BPH. If you are having any curious problems peeing check this out.

www.cancer.org/cancers/prostate

This is the American Cancer Society's Prostate Resource Center and they'll give you lots of man-to-man talk about your prostate. Next time they ask for a contribution you'll know what some of it's for.

www.cancerlinkusa.com/prostate/index.htm

A physician guided site for patients and their families.

www.hypertext.org/maintext.html#top

A superb, non commercial site created by a patient who did lots of research on the subject and presents virtually everything you want to know on the subject.

Guys our age are starting to realize that perhaps we are mortal after all and in the quest to tilt the odds more in our favor it's a good idea to stay informed about problems like prostate that are worrisome in our age group. A few are listed here with sites to inform, support and cure.

Sexually Transmitted Diseases

At your age you should know better, but in the event there are some funny rashes itching around your body this is the place to find out just what you may have caught. The good news, I suppose, is that you can still get it up.

www.mdchoice.com/Pt/PtInfo/std.asp

A brief explanation of various sexually transmitted diseases. The search boxes at the top of the site will give you more information than you want.

www.mediconsult.com

A comprehensive site that gives you information on everything that can go wrong. Just pick a condition that is troubling you and let the doctors fill you with fear.

www.condomania.com

Avoid trouble next time with one of this company's many styles of condoms. They even rate different brands.

www.healthanswers.com

Just click on STD and receive expert advice on so many scary diseases that you'll learn to keep your pants zipped.

www.healthlinkusa.com/276feat.htm

A very comprehensive site with a wide range of information and links to even more.

Vision Concerns

•••:• **ophthalmology.about.com**

An excellent overview on all the new eye surgery techniques. Search under "vision correction" on the bottom and if you can read it all you'll get an Ophthalmologist degree.

•••:• **www.asklasikdocs.com**

Board certified surgeons answer every possible question on Lasik surgery in great detail.

•••:• **www.lasersite.com**

Laser eye surgery explained and a directory of doctors who perform this surgery.

•••:• **www.ftc.gov/bcp/conline/pubs/health/vision.htm**

This government site has an excellent discussion of vision correction procedures. It really helps you to read between the lines of all the sites selling vision correction procedures.

•••:• **www.aoa.dhhs.gov/aoa/pages/agepages/eyes.html**

Aging and your eyes. Your government gives you the honest poop.

Can't see as well at night? Sick of your contact lenses or glasses? Been hearing about the new surgical vision correcting procedures? I for one have been interested for years but I've been a coward when it comes to sharp objects or lasers fooling with my eyes. In case you are braver, here is the place to learn more.

Weight Stuff and Nutrition

It's normal to gain a little weight as you grow older but there comes a time when you have to draw the line in the sand or end up being a fat old man. These sites will help you at least establish some bench marks about where you should be and what you should be eating to get there.

•••❖ **www.americanheart.org/Whats_News/ AHA_News_Releases/obesitytips.html**

Tips on finding a healthy weight for yourself from the American Heart Association. By the time, of course, that you've typed in this address you'll have lost a pound or two.

•••❖ **www.eatright.org/nfs/nfs51.html**

American Dietetic Assoc. answers questions on nutrition and fitness.

•••❖ **www.thriveonline.com/health/Library/ CAD/abstract1638.html**

Our life span is 7 years less than women's. Close the gap with the suggestions in this short article.

•••❖ **ianrwww.unl.edu/pubs/Foods/g1194.htm**

This nutrition guide for men was written by a woman who thinks we know what grams are.

•••❖ **top.monad.net/~vsi/java/bfc.html**

A body fat calculator. Try it. It's kind of fun.

Diets

•••: **www.catabolic.com**

> This diet claims to work 3 times faster than starvation. It's based on 100 foods that burn more calories, being digested, than they provide. It costs $19.95 to learn what they are.

•••: **www.dietinfo.com/diets.htm**

> This site lists a zillion diets, clinics and centers. If you follow each for a day you'll end up weighing nothing.

•••: **www.dietsite.com**

> A free service that will analyze your diet. They also talk about sport nutrition and alternative nutrition which seems to mean herbs.

•••: **www.obesity.com**

> A scary web address, Obesity.com Da da da dum, but there is very well presented information on health and weight loss and yes, a number to tell you if you are obese.

There are millions, maybe billions of diets on the web and in fact anytime your computer is working too slowly you can be sure it's because fat women are looking up more diets. Us guys don't really get fat. Perhaps portly and occasionally stout but at worst you can say our bodies are solid and any increase in weight makes us only more aerodynamically sound rather than fat. In case, however, you do want to lose a little weight here are a few sites that will help you.

Diets

Some of the diet sites on this page offer serious help. Others offer ridiculous fantasy. Now that you're over 50 I can assume you'll be able to pick out the difference and I'm including the ridiculous ones for your amusement.

www.cambridgediet.com

With the Cambridge Diet you buy and eat a lot of their goo and they promise you'll lose weight.

www.weightwatchers.com

Weight Watchers must work cause they have meetings all over the world. They offered to find one in your country and I picked a place named EESTI, God only knows where, and sure enough they had a Weight Watchers. What's more the site was in EESTIAN or whatever.

www.prevention.com/weight/wlwb

You just tell them what you'd like to weigh and they'll tell you just how many calories a day you can eat. The 71 weight loss tips are pretty good.

www.nutra-slim.com/mega4.html

This site is a scream. The special Accelerated Fat Burning diet lets you "burn up fat" even while you sleep. Mostly you'll just keep clicking on wild claims until you reach the $19.95 plus $4.85 shipping and handling finale.

www.oxycise.com

With this weight loss program you don't diet or take pills or buy gadgets. You just use oxygen. All you have to do is buy the videos, and breathe, and you'll be skinny in no time.

The Stuff You Eat and What It Does To You

•••❖ **www.navigator.tufts.edu**

This site performs a remarkable service in rating over 200 nutritional web sites based on accuracy, depth of information and usability.

•••❖ **www.mayohealth.org**

The Mayo Clinic's Health Oasis has a nutrition center that Tufts rated the highest. You might as well get your nutritional information from the best.

•••❖ **www.pueblo.gsa.gov**

According to the Tufts rating your government is on the stick here with an excellent site that gives good information on food and its effect on your health.

•••❖ **vm.cfsan.fda.gov/list.html**

A complex and serious site but if you have a particular subject in mind here is where you get the real advice. Look up, for example, Health Claims On Food.

•••❖ **www.ama-assn.org/consumer.htm**

The AMA Health Insight is a very useable site with excellent information on everything you should or shouldn't stick in your stomach. You have to believe them, they're your doctors.

•••❖ **www.cyberdiet.com**

A fun site with all the tools you need to plan a healthful diet. Check out the fast food quest and see what you are really eating.

When you get to be 50 you can no longer eat and drink with abandon. You start to carry antacid pills everywhere and no longer sleep well if you eat bratwurst and cream pies after 9 PM. These sites will give you some idea of what's good for you and not, if you haven't already figured it out.

Fitness

More exercise. That's the one thing all the magazines insist will extend your life and you never see an article disputing it 6 months later. So get with it and I hope you'll find a little inspiration from some of these sites.

www.fitnesslink.com

A neat site with all sorts of information on exercise, nutrition, gyms and even a pin up of the week.

www.mensfitness.com

The site for Men's Fitness magazine which has some pretty good information on training, nutrition, health and gear.

www.acefitness.org

This site lists 40,000 certified personal trainers. One of them has to be cute enough to inspire you to exercise more.

www.primusweb.com/fitnesspartner/ library/libindex.htm

Excellent equipment and book reviews. Check this out before you spend money.

www.pitt.edu/~pahnet

The Physical Activity and Health network tells you how beneficial exercise is with basic articles from the leading sources. You've probably heard all this before and just didn't listen.

Vasectomy

•••• **www.plannedparenthood.org/BIRTH-CONTROL/allaboutvas.htm**

Everything about Vasectomies from Planned Parenthood. Who are these "planners"?

•••• **www.geocities.com/fl_cheshire**

A vasectomy forum for men to discuss experiences and issues.

•••• **www.vasectomy.ca**

This site describes a "no scalpel" vasectomy plus has an excellent discussion of the general advisability of the procedure. Anything that avoids a scalpel is worth looking into.

•••• **oncolink.upenn.edu/pdq/600326.html**

This study examines increased risk of prostate cancer after a vasectomy. Something you'll want to check out.

•••• **www.gynpages.com/ultimate/vasectomy.html**

Some good links on this site about the "ultimate birth control" method.

The very mention of this word terrifies me, but it is hailed as one of the safest and easiest birth control methods. Well, at least until recently when a few reports have surfaced about it possibly causing some kind of prostate or cancer problems. I can't remember. Wait a few weeks and another study will refute it anyway.

Tattoo Removal

At 50 you may be interested in removing some of the indiscretions of youth. Here are some places that give information on tattoo removal or if you've never had a tattoo perhaps you can try one knowing they're not as permanent as they used to be.

www.patient-info.com/tattoo.htm

An excellent discussion of the different methods of tattoo removal. The laser ones are the only that don't appear to hurt.

www.lasersociety.org

Laser tattoo, scar and wrinkle removal with before and after pictures.

www.removal.webhost.com.au/index1.html

This is a rather complete discussion of one man's tattoo removal experience.

www.undoyourtattoo.com

This clinic explains how removal is done and answers questions.

www.tattoomd.com

A board certified physician explains tattoo removal and shows excellent photos.

www.tattooz.com/tattoo_sites.htm

If all the talk about removal has got you interested in getting a tattoo this site offers links to some very impressive artists.

lcohol

content.health.msn.com/content/article/1674.50182

Information when alcohol becomes a problem.

www.alcoholics-anonymous.org

If you have friends who need help Alcoholics-Anonymous is the place to send them.

www.ncadd.org

The National Council on Alcohol and Drug Dependence. Don't let the picture of the founder scare you, there is good information here.

alcoholism.miningco.com/health/alcoholism

Links to a billion (well maybe a hundred) alcohol-problem related areas.

www.health.org

A real lot of information from the National Clearinghouse for Alcohol and Drug Information. If you read all of this you'll have no time left to drink.

Alcohol can be a real health problem. Too much that is. A little is supposed to be good at least this month. Mostly the people who are having trouble with their drinking won't admit it so this page probably will do little good but perhaps you have a friend....

Compulsive Gambling

Gambling like drinking is not something with which you ever see yourself having a problem. View a few of these sites, just for fun, and you may get to know yourself a little better.

mayohealth.org/mayo/9712/htm/gambling.htm

Help from the experts at the Mayo clinic on this 500 billion dollar a year problem.

www.intervention.com/gambling

When to intervene with someone who may have a gambling problem.

www.ncpgambling.org

The National Council on Gambling has 10 questions to ask yourself.

www.gamblersanonymous.org

Gamblers Anonymous home page.

www.slotland.com/?p=334500

In case you're not having a problem, this site lets you play the slots. Have fun.

lternative Medicine

•••• **homeopathic-md-do.com**

This is a national list of real MD's who practice classical homeopathy which as I understand it consists of giving you an extremely diluted form of a poison in an appropriate dose matched to the poison that is making you sick. Or something like that.

•••• **www.powerfate.com**

This product, for only $39.95, claims to actually make good luck happen. It works by absorbing all the "negatives" in your life. In case it doesn't work there is a Power Enhancer for only an additional $9. And a money back guarantee no less. Don't miss this site if you need good luck.

•••• **spiritualnetwork.com/links/New**

You can click on this site for actual divine insights ($70 per hour) and links to such diverse "medical treatments" as Hemp Oil, Tarot readings, Shazam Astrology, Aumara Light and Healing circles and other things that defy human comprehension.

•••• **www.lisco.com/wuebben/TM/health.html**

Maharishi Vedic creates heaven on earth with this website of bliss and enlightenment.

If you hate to go to doctors or if you don't trust doctors or if the doctors haven't been able to cure what ails you, there is always alternative medicine to turn to. With alternative medicine you can often get totally untrained quacks and dangerous unsanitary nuts to do ridiculous things to your body. The funny thing is sometimes these treatments work. Who am I to knock them. Some kinds of alternative medicine have even entered mainstream health care. You can read about alternative treatments here and make your own judgments.

Memory

At 50 you haven't lost it yet but you are starting to see the signs of forgetfulness. Now, where did I put those car keys, and what did I go into the garage for and "his name is on the tip of my tongue". So here are some sites to help cope with the problem before you become a babbling idiot and can't find the way to the toilet.

www.epub.org.br/cm/n01/memo/memory.htm

The mechanisms of memory, the loss of memory and how to improve your memory. There are two important ways. One is to relax. I forget the other.

piebald.princeton.edu/mb427/1997/students/learning/people.html

A concise introduction to human memory. Like, if, for example, you can remember this site's address.

www.exploratorium.edu/memory/dont_forget

Games and activities to test your memory and techniques to help you improve it.

www.memoryzine.com

You can purchase a course on CD's to help improve your memory. They're not cheap but neither is forgetting your secret Swiss Bank account number.

www.markgiles.co.uk/methods.html

Secrets that magicians use and you can learn to improve your memory. They include rhyming, chains, familiar route, and other methods that are all nicely explained.

Sleeping

www.sleep-sdca.com

This sleep disorder site sure lists a load of sleeping problems. It's enough to make you lose sleep. Take the self-test. You'll probably fall asleep before you reach question 30.

www.ninds.nih.gov/patients/disorder/ sleep/brain-basics-sleep.htm

Lots of sleep information here though the sleeping tips are pretty obvious.

www.newtechpub.com/phantom

Let Phantom Sleep Resources (there's a name that inspires confidence) handle your sleep problems. Find out if you have Apnea, whatever that is, and try not to lose sleep worrying about it.

www.supertips.com/fw/1067.htm

For only $6.95 they'll sell you a book with 67 good ways to sleep. Me? I just stick a pillow over my head.

www.nshsleep.com/test.cfm

Take this test from Northside Hospital's Sleep Medicine Institute and send it to them. You'll get feedback on your responses. Ask for a second opinion.

If you're like me you no longer can sleep till noon. In fact, you have trouble sleeping through the night and getting up to pee every now and then is becoming a very necessary thing to do. Well these sites just might give you some ideas on how sleep works and how you can perhaps "sleep like a baby" again.

Snoring

Does your mate and even people in the next room complain about your snoring? Does your snoring even wake you up? Well, when that happens it's time to do something about it. These sites all tell you snoring is not a funny problem so don't think this is just a joke.

www.snoring-strips.com

This site sells "chin up breathing strips" which you stick around your jaw and hope no one sees you while you sleep cause you look pretty ridiculous. They swear it helps.

www.snoringless.com

For 20 bucks you spray this stuff in your throat and it lubricates the snoring spot so everything is quiet.

www.snoring-help.com/index.html

This site sounds like real doctors that treat serious snoring with surgery and radio frequency waves as well as snoring help appliances.

hometown.aol.com/roctex69/myhomepage/index.html

Here's a good solution. This site sells some sort of electronic earplug that you give to whoever is complaining about your snoring. Then the whole problem is off your back.

www.snaplab.com/infosn1.htm

Snap Laboratories sends you a recording device to record your snoring which they analyze, if you can believe it, and send to your doctor who then cuts your throat out (just kidding).

Dentists

•••• **www.dental-implants.com**

If you are going to have an implant it's a good idea to read this page and learn something about the procedure. The cost can range from $500 to $6,000 per implant so at least look around a little to try to find one of the $500 kind that don't rust.

•••• **www.dentistinfo.com**

Find a dentist, lists of dental terms but best of all frequently asked questions like "what exactly is a root canal" but you really don't want to know.

•••• **www.dentistdirectory.com**

You can get email answers to all your dental questions here for free. It's a lot better than going to have someone drill holes in your teeth.. But in case these e-mails don't stop the problem, there is also a directory of dentists.

•••• **www.toothinfo.com**

This is a great public service site with no sponsors. The Dental Consumer Advisor gives lots of health facts about dentistry, great diagrams and even an article on "How Honest Are Dentists".

•••• **www.dentalfear.org**

If you're scared to death of dentists this is the site you need. It deals with dental phobia and how you can handle it short of flossing after each meal so you never have to go to the dentist.

People sometimes call this the gold and silver age of our lives. Unfortunately much of this gold and silver is in our teeth. We've learned not to bite down too hard on pretzels and not to open tough pistachio nuts with our teeth. Though I debated putting such a terrifying subject in the book I'm spending more and more time with dentists and they said they'd charge me less if I gave them a pitch.

Mental Health

These are the sites that will let you know if indeed your family is driving you crazy. I've found that by the time you're 50, however crazy or not you may be, you're pretty satisfied with your personality and not too interested in changing it. Perhaps you can use these sites to prove to yourself just how nutty everyone else is.

www.mentalhelp.net

An award winning online guide to mental health and psychiatry. They even have a mental health store with herbs and stuff to make you better.

www.metanoia.org/choose/index.html

Sound advice on choosing a mental help therapist in case life just doesn't seem to be working or you are hurting inside.

depression.about.com/health/depression

An extensive guide to depression and information on causes, defining it, treatment, and much more.

www.mentalhealth.com

An encyclopedia of mental health information. The most common disorders are listed with description, diagnosis and treatment. Enough links to absolutely everything about the subject to truly drive you crazy.

www.mhsource.com/expert

This professor of psychiatry at Tufts provides a free service that will answer your e-mail questions.

Recurring Dreams

•••• **redrival.com/nightmare/dictionary.html**

Your online dream dictionary can help you remember and explain your dreams, if you dare. Most unpleasant dreams seem to have a basis in insecurity.

•••• **dreams.nsm.it/dreams/varie/bears.html**

Tell this site about your dreams and they will try to interpret them. I'm not so sure I'd want them to.

•••• **www.shpm.com/articles/dreams/index.shtml**

Self Help and Psychology magazine has some wonderful articles on using dreams to improve your life.

•••• **1st-spot.freeservers.com/topic_dreams.html**

A great list of sites about dreams. If you start checking these out you'll have no time left for sleeping.

•••• **www.lifetreks.com**

These people do research into dreams and need your dreams. You can give at the office (if you nap there) and also at home. Fun lists of other people's dreams.

Do you still have that dream about final exams? You know the one where you have to pass this course to graduate and you haven't been to a single class all year. A version that I sometimes have is being unable to find the exam room. Well, join the club and learn about other people who suffer the same way and maybe even learn what to do about it.

Indigestion

By the time you're 50 you'll understand just which foods are incompatible with your gastrointestinal system. Still if you really love those onions or peppers or salami or beans the occasional discomfort may be worth the taste especially if there is something you can take for it.

www.naturalhealthconsult.com/ulcers.html

A good discussion of indigestion and a whole list of natural and medical products to treat the problem.

www.healthtouch.com/level1/leaflets/ 118977/118977.htm

A very comprehensive site that covers a long list of stomach and digestion problems.

www.egregore.com/herb/Indigestion.htm

A guide to about 50 medicinal herbs and which will help your stomach problems.

4indigestion.4anything.com

A large resource with alternative medicine answers to your stomach problems but also doctor links.

www.1001herbs.com/menus/Poor_Digestion.html

A long, long list of herbs to treat indigestion. If you try all of these you'll weigh 400 lbs.

S ex Drive

•••⫶ **www.mens-page.com**

This site deals with impotence and male menopause. The stories are frightening and I recommend skipping this site if you have hypochondriac tendencies.

•••⫶ **www.pickupwomen.net**

Nature's secret weapon; pheromones, whatever that is, and it's guaranteed and only $21.95 and comes with a free book, "How To Seduce Girls".

•••⫶ **www.sexnaturally.com**

This Chinese herb mixture fixes absolutely every sexual problem known to man (and woman). It contains amongst other ingredients, Cictanche, Fenugreek and Epimedium. How can it miss.

•••⫶ **www.baaaa.com/adnet/eros3.htm**

"Put the lead back in your pencil" with Eros Sex Drive Enhancer. Who knows, if you believe it'll work maybe it'll work. I'd rather eat clams.

•••⫶ **neuro-www.mgh.harvard.edu/forum_2/ EpilepsyF /sexdrive.html**

The Department of Neurology at Mass. General Hospital maintains this forum on sex drive and they should know what they're talking about.

Now I am sure none of my readers have had any problem with their sex drive but just in case you have "a friend" who isn't doing too well you could direct him to these sites.

Prescriptions Online

These prescription sites purport to save you the embarrassment of going to your real doctor and admitting you can't get it up or are so vain you worry about going bald. Better hurry and get your order in. I suspect the FDA is going to put these people out of business before too long.

www.impotenceprescriptions.com

Here is the place to get Viagra online with only a $75 "medical examination" fee the first time.

www.centerformenshealth.com

Get Viagra, Propecia, growth hormones and all the other magic you've always wanted.

www.friendlypharmacy.com

Viagra for $4 per dose once you've paid the $50 "online doctor" fee.

www.doctorsrxmedical.com

This service is so private it's located in the Bahamas. Thirty Viagra tablet for about $10 each with "medical consulting". That should last you a month.

www.drugs-express.com

You'll be back in action within 24 hours with their fast shipping and $4.50 per Viagra pill cost.

oga

•••⦂ **www.yogasite.com**

An eclectic collection of yoga connections. It gives the postures and describes a dozen styles that will confuse you no end.

•••⦂ **www.yogaclass.com**

A lovely site with a free online yoga class. Here is an easy way to get started with no cost or embarrassment.

•••⦂ **www.will-harris.com/yoga**

Yoga exercises you can do at your desk. You'll feel great but your co-workers will think you've lost your marbles.

•••⦂ **www.santosha.com/asanas/asana.html**

Instructions on a long list of yoga poses. Pronouncing the names looks as difficult as bending 50 year old bodies into the position.

•••⦂ **www.sivananda.org**

This award winning site has 345 pages. Read it all and you probably won't be able to stand up.

At 50 I'm finding my flexibility is starting to go and I was never flexible enough to afford to lose any. People our age who are into yoga can bend themselves into pretzels. There must be something to it.

Travel for 50 Year Olds

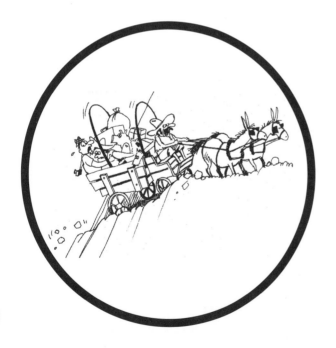

Look, you're 50. If you don't see the world now just when are you going to do it? The time to take all those trips you've been dreaming about is while you have your health and the ability to really enjoy them. This section has a bunch of pages that make travel planning and travel arrangements easy. The following 2 pages list the online sites of most major American and foreign airlines.

U.S. Airline Sites

•••:	Aloha Airlines	www.alohaair.com
•••:	Alaska Airlines	www.alaskaair.com
•••:	American Airlines	www.AA.com
•••:	American West Airlines	www.americawest.com
•••:	Continental Airlines	www.continental.com
•••:	Delta Airlines	www.delta-air.com
•••:	Frontier Airline	www.flyfrontier.com
•••:	Hawaiian Airlines	www.hawaiianair.com
•••:	Midway Air	www.midwayair.com
•••:	Northwest Airlines	www.nwa.com
•••:	Southwest Airlines	www.southwest.com
•••:	TransWorld Airline	www.twa.com
•••:	United Airlines	www.ual.com
•••:	US Airways	www.usairways.com

To make reservations, find out schedules and most important get the extra frequent flier miles, book your flight on these sites.

Foreign Airlines

Some of these airlines offer the best service in the world and some save money by not bothering to service their engines. You figure out which.

Aer Lingus	www.aerlingus.ie
Air Canada	www.aircanada.ca
Air France	www.airfrance.com
Air India	www.airindia.com
Air New Zealand	www.airnz.com
All Nippon Airways	svc.ana.co.jp/eng
British Airways	www.british-airways.com
Cathay Pacific	www.cathaypacific.com
ElAl Airlines	www.elal.co.il/homepage.htm
Finnair	www.finnair.com
Iberian Airlines	www.iberia.com/ingles/home.html
Iceland Air	www.icelandair.com
Japanese Airline	www.jal.co.jp/english/index_e.html
KLM Airlines	www.klm.com
Korean Air	www.koreanair.com
Lufthansa	www.lufthansa.com
Mexicana Airlines	www.mexicana.com.mx/mx2/english/home.asp
Olympic Airlines	www.olympic-airways.gr
Quantas Airwaya	www.qantas.com.au
Sabena Airways	www.sabena-usa.com
Swissair	www.swissair.com
TAP Airlines (Portugal)	www.tap-airportugal.pt/en/index1.html
VARIG Airlines	www.varig.com.br/english/rghome-p.htm
Virgin Atlantic	www.fly.virgin.com

Travel Books Online

•••• www.fodors.com

•••• www.frommers.com

•••• www.lonelyplanet.com

•••• travel.roughguides.com

•••• www.wtgonline.com/navigate/world.asp

•••• www.zagat.com

While these sites don't always give you the entire book (let them make a living) you can get an incredible amount of information about virtually every tourist location in the world. It is the smart place to look when you start planning a trip.

Worldwide Health Warnings and Information

If you're going to take a great vacation or trip the last thing you want is to die from some horrible disease that creeps up from your bare feet and infects your brain with a worm or worse. Likewise, most folk would rather not be kidnapped by mustached banditos who cut off ears for ransom. Check out these warning sites before making your non-refundable reservations.

www.who.int/emc/outbreak_news
Find out about the black plague before you leave.

www.cdc.gov/travel
Health requirements and medication recommendations for anywhere in the world.

travel.state.gov/travel_warnings.html
Travel warnings that even the CIA listens to.

www.tripprep.com/index.html
General trip information, health precautions, disease risk summary, official health data, and US advisories.

www.pathfinder.com/travel/TL/links/health.html
Links to multiple health sites. Everything from diving medicine to high altitude sickness.

Travel Clothing

•••⦂ **www.exofficio.com**

The ultimate clothing in which to see the world. Men's clothing sorted by traveling needs such as evening out, stay warm, stay dry, in transit, active, urban.

•••⦂ **www.tilley.com**

This Canadian company has some fun customs you're supposed to carry out when you meet someone else wearing their stuff.

•••⦂ **www.travelsmith.com**

I have personally used this company a great deal and have never been sorry.

•••⦂ **www.fibronet.com.tw/wool/finepacking.html**

This site tells you how to pack. It's pretty basic stuff but in case you haven't traveled since the boy scouts it might be a good review.

•••⦂ **www.llbeam.com**

L.L. Bean where not only can you get travel clothes but also the pack to stuff them in.

You don't want to look like a geek when you are representing your country overseas, do you? Better get some of these wrinkle resistant, washable wonders from companies that specialize in travel wear. These clothes will also help you blend in with all the other tourists so the natives won't mistake you for someone with whom their family has a blood feud.

ctive Vacations for 50 Year Olds

You've been to Europe, seen the States, recognize the hazards of too much sun on a beach and gained weight on cruises. Perhaps now you're ready for active vacations. These will take you to more remote places and teach you new things that you need to stay alive like Eskimo rolling your kayak, boiling your water, shaking deadly insects out of your boot. You'll come home needing a week in bed before going back to work.

www.gorp.com/akdisc.htm
Alaska adventure trips. White water rafting, hiking, canoeing etc.

www.belize.com/reef%2Dscuba.html
Scuba diving and snorkeling in Belize on their barrier reef.

www.goski.com
Your ski vacation site.

courseguide.golfweb.com
This is a good guide to golf courses around the world.

www.greatoutdoors.com/index.html
Great outdoor activities of all kinds with links to equipment and ratings.

www.away.com
A travel company that specializes in adventure travel.

Active vacations for 50 year olds

- **www.serendipityadventures.com/rugged.htm**
  Rafting, hiking, climbing, biking and more in Costa Rica.

- **www.fodors.com/sports/**
  Over 500 sport and adventure trips in North America from sky diving to covered wagon trips.

- **www.llamatours.com**
  Llama tours in British Columbia. Let the llamas carry your gear.

- **www.beachs%2Dmca.com**
  Spend your vacation seeing the world from the back of a motorcycle.

- **www.outsidemag.com**
  Outside Magazine's site with destinations for active trips around the world.

- **www.spectrav.com**
  Adventure and special interest travel links to the operators of everything from dog sled to cattle drive.

- **activetravel.about.com**
  A network of sites about all sorts of active trips plus every other kind.

On many of these trips you'll be mixing with people much younger than you are. This is a great way to keep thinking and being young. An old man I met skiing once said that to keep young you need 3 things after good genes. You have to be optimistic, athletic and heroic. By heroic I think he meant doing idiotic things like rappelling off a mountain or dog sledding in the arctic.

Exotic Vacation Travel

If you are not going to wildly exotic spots now, when will you be able to? Retirement, you'll say, is a good time but by then your back or knees will be acting up and you won't enjoy yourself. 50 is a fine time to start seeing all those places you've been dreaming about and here are a few sites to whet your appetite.

www.aandktours.com/html/index.html

Abercrombie and Kent's site. Check out the Marco Polo Club for remote and exotic locations.

www.lonelyplanet.com/dest/dest.htm

Lonely Planet's in-depth descriptions of exotic locations.

www.hotwired.com/rough

This is the Rough Guide's site which gives information on exotic locations (14,000 they claim) around the world. The information is very detailed and complete.

www.africaarchipelago.com/home.html

This London agency specializes in travel to East Africa.

www.tourism-asia.com

The insider's guide to travel throughout Asia.

www.virtualnorth.net

Just type in the kind of arctic vacation you want and they will come up with the outfitters. Do they bring portable toilets?

Nude Resorts and Beaches

•••• **www.tanr.com**

The Trade Association for Nude Recreation with quite extensive lists of resorts plus newsletters and the usual rationalizations of why being naked is so great. You know, the completely free feeling, the natural healthy experience, the fresh air, getting to see lots of naked women.

•••• **www.bareaffair.com**

This company books travel arrangements to nude and clothing optional resorts around the world.

•••• **www.dbphoto.co.nz**

This New Zealand site lists nude resorts, beaches, clubs etc. and has lots of pictures so don't open this site unless you're ready for it. Oh yeah, and they sell lots of naturalist videos.

•••• **www.bluebonnetnudistpark.com/baredare**

The Bare As You Dare 5K cross-country race. Get fit and run around naked at the same time.

•••• **http://www.ctc-online.com/nudelink.htm**

The "most comprehensive" naturalist information available for a mere $2.99 per minute. Seems to me there are less expensive ways to find a nude beach.

Let's face it. You're 50 years old and have never been to a nude beach. Don't you think it's about time? Here is a list of some and I bet you can find one not too far from where you live (or perhaps you'd prefer one really far from where you live).

Nude resorts and beaches

I had such a good time doing this research that I thought I'd list a few more.

• • • **www.sfbg.com/Nude/index.html**

A directory of California nude beaches. Find the ones where all the stars hang out.

• • • **www.nudebeachguide.com**

Nude beaches of the Northeast. Can you believe, even in New England?

• • • **sffb.com**

South Florida nude beaches. I thought they were all nude in South Miami.

• • • **www.aanr.com**

The American Association For Nude Recreation is surely looking for 50 year old guys to join and expand the intellectual horizons of the organization. Along with other advice they explain that it's proper nude etiquette to always carry your own towel to sit upon.

• • • **www.e-s-a.com**

The Eastern Sunbathing Association has a directory, by state, of clubs and resorts in the Eastern U.S.

Gambling Junkets

- **www.casinotours.com**

  This travel company organizes gambling junkets to casinos all around the U.S. and Caribbean.

- **www.casinojunkets.com**

  Casino junkets to Costa Rica.

- **www.4casino.com/links.htm**

  If you want to gamble this site has a handicapping service, junkets, computer gambling directory and more.

- **www.pokerandcasino.com/poker.htm**

  Serious poker playing in Costa Rica and casino gambling as well.

- **www.americasline.com**

  The odds and point spreads and all the information you need to make the right choices.

- **www.gambling-systems.com/books.html**

  Gambling books online. If you are going to be losing money you might as well know the odds.

- **www.smartgaming.com/index.htm**

  The Gambling Digest with articles and tips and systems.

As long as you don't have a gambling problem as discussed under the health section you're allowed to go into these sites and plan a gambling junket. If you become a big player I hear the casinos pick up the tabs for all your travel. Good luck.

Sports

Sports are to guys what snuggling and talk after sex is to women. We love sports. We love watching them and playing them and the only change with being 50 is that we may spend more time watching instead of playing. Not too many 50 year old men still participate in tackle football games. In truth after participating in almost any sport, other than golf, we tend to spend the next few days relaxing with Advil and hot baths. Still the interest is there and these sport sites will allow you to keep up with whatever level of detailed information you'd like.

Golf

•••• **www.golfweb.com**

Golf lessons online along with lots of tournament information, gear ratings, and a pro shop.

•••• **www.golfcourse.com**

Reviews on over 16,000 courses. "So much golf so little time."

•••• **golfcircuit.com/cgi-bin/datasearch/bottom.html**

Stats from the circuit, instruction, a golf search engine, plus the inevitable pro shop.

•••• **www.msnbc.com/news/golf1_front.asp**

NBC Sport's golf coverage with all the latest results.

•••• **www.pgaonline.com**

The official PGA site with audio coverage of the championships.

•••• **golf.traveller.com/golf**

Traveler's golf information center with 2,000 courses, scorecard archives, and golf associations.

Of all the activities suited to 50 year olds, golf is one of the best. While the psychological frustration level can be extreme, the physical stress level is safe, the camaraderie superb and you can win lots of money if you play with a bunch of turkeys. These sites will keep you up-to-date with the sport as well as providing information on courses all over the world.

Golf Equipment

Buying the equipment is as much fun as playing to many guys and finding the latest club that is going to enhance your game or the ball guaranteed not to hook probably occupies more of these people's time than lessons. If you're one of them, and I count myself among you, these sites will be a joy.

www.golfandtennisworld.com

Golf and Tennis equipment. They promise lowest prices and over 20,000 items in stock. No way you could lose that many balls.

www.mvp.com

High quality golf and other sports equipment along with expert advice on what to buy.

www.clubstest.com

They claim unbiased ratings of all golf clubs plus up to the minute tournament stats and leaderboards.

www.mygolf.com

They sure have a load of golf products and claim the lowest prices on the web.

www.golfcoop.com

This is a non profit coop of golfers who have banded together to get the best prices for their group. You have to register before getting the prices.

Golf Magazines

www.golfdigest.com

Golf Digest's online site with more golf information than you can use.

www.golftoday.co.uk

Europe's premier online golf magazine.

www.golfmagazine.com

Golf Magazine's online site. If you have a day too rainy to play you can easily spend it surfing this site.

www.seniorgolfer.com

I don't know if we are seniors yet but if we are here is a magazine just for you.

www.golfandtravel.com

There are some incredibly beautiful photos on this site and you are going to want to visit them.

www.golfillustrated.com

There seem to be more golf magazines than telephone solicitors at dinner time. The sites don't carry the entire publication but you can probably glean all the information you'll ever need by just scanning several of them. It makes me wonder who bothers to subscribe when so much is available for free.

www.golftips.com

Some pretty good tips on improving your game.

www.travelandleisuregolf.com

Who has time to play golf when all these magazines are vying for your attention.

There are many golf magazines and in addition to news about the sport they are a wonderful source for tips on improving your game. I for one could never get anything out of pictures of swings and hip rotations and weight shifts but perhaps you can understand this stuff.

Fishing

There is a peace and beauty in fishing that combines with the excitement of the chase which makes it one of the favorite pastimes of men. When you are over 50 your brains should have developed enough to at least match those of a stupid fish. An additional benefit is that fishing activities rarely require chiropractic care.

www.fishandgame.com

A comprehensive site that delivers fish reports, articles, travel and marketplace information.

www.flyfishingjournal.com

Tips, product reviews, fly tying, stream reports and lots more.

www.flyshop.com

Online fishing magazine with good articles, fish reports, classifieds, tide tables, etc.

www.acc.umu.se/~widmark/lwmanufa.html

A list of a zillion fishing equipment manufacturers. Just click on any one and you'll usually find their whole line. An incredible site.

fishingequipment.com

This site has links to absolutely every kind of fishing equipment and every kind of fishing site imaginable. Go here -you don't need me.

Fly Fishing

••••• **flyfishing.com**

This very comprehensive resource has information on tying, shops, books, classifieds, lodges and more.

••••• **flyfishing.about.com/sports/flyfishing**

Everything you need to know to find and catch them.

••••• **www.azlink.com/~jshannon/flygloss.html**

Fly fishing glossary of terms. Now you have to learn all these words.

••••• **www.myhost.com/flyfishing101**

A beginner's guide to fly fishing equipment, techniques, tying and more.

••••• **www.flyfishamerica.com**

Online edition of Fly Fish America Magazine with lots of excellent articles.

••••• **www.flyshop.com**

This online magazine has loads of stories and directories.

This is the "in" sport of the 90's. Everyone is fly fishing and here you have a sport that combines the outdoor excitement of the chase with the finesse and skill of an artist. Besides that you can tie your own flies on rainy afternoons and feel real "arts and crafty."

Football

Here is a sport that has taken over most fan's Sundays and Monday nights not to even mention college games on Saturday. Where else can you enjoy a beer, relive your high school football days, watch a game and make money as well if you get the point spread right.

www.msnbc.com/news/NFL_Front.asp
The latest NFL news from MSNBC.

www.dickbutkus.com/dbfn
Dick Butkis Football Network covering everything from NFL to Pop Warner.

www.nflplayers.com
NFL players home pages, analysis and news.

www.sportserver.com/SportServer/football
Football news, college and professional.

www.ultimatefootballshop.com
The ultimate football shop where you can buy authentic football apparel from Sports Illustrated and the NFL.

www.cnnsi.com/football/college/conferences/acc
Sports Illustrated and CNN combine to offer team profiles, scores, news, statistics standings and schedules.

Baseball

••• **www.msnbc.com/news/MLB_Front.asp**
   The latest baseball news from MSNBC.

••• **www.baseball.com**
   Scores, news, team web sites, everything.

••• **www.heavyhitter.com/default.asp**
   This baseball search engine will help you find
   anything about the game.

••• **www.totalbaseball.com**
   The official baseball encyclopedia with statistics,
   player profiles, history, chat, store and whatever.

••• **www.usatoday.com/sports/mlb.htm**
   The latest news, standings, statistics etc.

It's still the all-American pastime and by God when we were young we played baseball and not some new fangled soccer, volleyball or lacrosse game. It's still something to enjoy as we remember our own games and the splendid times watching the pro's at the ballparks before the days of televised games.

Baseball

Baseball lets you remember little league and uniforms and wood bats and getting stuck in right field cause you were the worst player on the team. At least that's where they put me.

www.baseballhalloffame.org
Here you can visit here the National Baseball Hall of Fame.

www.fastball.com
Scores updated every 3 minutes and listen in on the dial if you can't catch the game.

www.majorleaguebaseball.com
The official site of Major League Baseball. Schedules, scores stats, team profiles and all the rest.

www.sportingnews.com/baseball/sluggers
A list of baseball's 50 greatest sluggers from Sporting News.

www.minorleaguebaseball.com
All the minor league baseball news for 50 year olds who can't get enough with the majors.

Basketball

••••• **www.basketball.com**

Everything about basketball from the NBA to the cheerleader of the day.

••••• **www.msnbc.com/msn/NBA2.asp?cp1=1**

Current news about the NBA from MSNBC.

••••• **www.usabasketball.com**

The men's and women's national teams as well as Olympic information.

••••• **www.finalfour.net**

The official site of the NCAA basketball championships.

••••• **cnnsi.com/basketball/college**

CNN and Sports Illustrated coverage of men's and women's college basketball.

••••• **hwww.hoophall.com**

Basketball's Hall of Fame with all the exhibits, stories and history.

••••• **www.bbhighway.com**

A site for coaches to improve their skill along with all the usual information about games and players.

You don't necessarily bet and they don't often get bloody so basketball must be the intellectual major sport that appeals to the more sophisticated 50 year olds among us as well as those over 6' tall who did well in the game when 6' meant something.

Hockey

The speed of the game alone has a tremendous appeal and the action and amazing hand eye coordination has many claiming that this is the most athletic of the major sports. The fights, while less than in the old days, are great to watch especially if you don't get boxing on your cable.

•••• **www.hockey.com**
Hockey news, stats, scores and everything.

•••• **proicehockey.about.com/sports/proicehockey**
Scores, news, player profiles, and fights.

•••• **www.thn.com**
Online edition of The Hockey News.

•••• **www.nhl.com**
The official NHL site with stats, news, scores and history.

•••• **www.hockeydb.com**
An archive of hockey information dating back to the 1920's.

•••• **www.inthecrease.com**
Comprehensive coverage of major, minor and international hockey.

Boating

••• www.boating.com

Tides and tips, weather, buoys and boat shows. An all purpose boating site.

••• www.usps.org/usps.html

The United States Power Squadron.

••• www.powerboatmag.com

Online edition of Powerboat magazine with ratings, boating news and classifieds.

••• www.boatshow.com

This is like a super boat show online. The equivalent of 2,000 pages of details on boats and equipment.

••• www.boater.com

Charter, repairs, tips, books, classifieds.

••• www.allaboutboats.com

Boats for sale, boating events, fishing and lots of links to more boating information.

••• www.motorboatingandsailing.com

Excerpts from Motor Boating and Sail magazine with tips, equipment reviews and links.

••• www.boatfacts.com/home.asp

Articles are available from a dozen boating magazines plus classifieds, specs and other information.

Get yourself a captain's cap because when you are 50 and the wind's in your face you'll make a striking captain. The boat's needs may dominate your free time and suck up money like the hole in the water it is but when you are out on the blue with the wind in your face you feel a very happy man indeed.

Boating

You'll have no idea how many friends you have until you buy a boat. Whether water skiing, fishing or just cruising around everyone will accept your invitations. You will, of course, still have to do all the dirty and difficult maintenance yourself.

www.usedboatsonline.com

Schedule of boat shows plus a database of boats for sale.

www.woodenboat.com

Wooden Boat Magazine's home site with lots of information about these traditional beauties.

www.boatbiz.com

Designed for boating industry professionals this magazine has reviews and buyer's guide.

www.fishnfun.com

Purchase new or used boats online. Check for leaks later.

www.oz.net/~papillon/kbmanual/ colregs.html

The International Regulations for the Prevention of Collisions at Sea. Read this before you buy your boat. Please.

www.boatingsafety.com

Safety tips, info on tides, and advice on buying.

www.rngend.com

International Nautical Library with links to vast resources.

Sailing

- **sailing.about.com/sports/sailing/index.htm**

  Links to everything about sailing from about.com.

- **www.sailnet.com**

  Hundreds of articles and resources for the sailor.

- **www.yachtworld.com**

  A boating yellow pages with 17,000 marine businesses. Truly everything is here. Thousands of boats for sale.

- **www.sailnet.com/sailing**

  Sailing Magazine home site with some articles available from each issue.

- **www.sailingworld.com/swdeckpg.htm**

  Cruising and Sailing World online magazine with race reports, calendar and racing information.

- **www.american-sailing.com**

  American Sailing Assoc. with books and schools and standards for the sport.

- **sailing.info-access.com**

  Marine weather and tide information, sailors bulletin board, discussion groups and race calendars.

Sailing itself isn't really difficult. It's learning all the nautical terms that's a bitch. While you may think the wind's power is free you'll realize differently when you buy a sailboat and start replacing sails and lost winch handles.

Biking

It's your choice. You can be efficient with an aerodynamic position, hard seat, stiff bike and sore body or comfy with an upright position and plush equipment. Though I used to race seriously, now that I'm 50 I find myself bending, reluctantly, in the direction of comfort. You probably will also.

www.biking.com

Ten thousand bike products for sale plus biking articles and people.

www.dfwnetmall.com/cybersports/bicycle.htm

An introduction to biking for novices including buying a bike, maintenance and other information.

www.bicyclingmagazine.com

Online version of the leading biking magazine.

www.cycling.org

This is quite a site and can link you to any manufacturer as well as directions to any bike shop.

www.backroads.com

Backroads offers the largest and among the best bike tours worldwide.

www.gorp.com/gorp/activity/biking/bik_guid.htm

An excellent guide to bike trails and tours throughout the U.S.

www.sevencycles.com

They are expensive, but these guys make the best custom bikes in the world. I own one.

R unning

•••• **www.running.com**
This site leads you to just about everything you could ever need to know about running.

•••• **www.americanrunning.org**
The American Running Assoc. hosts a terrific site that lets you easily find information on all aspects of running, equipment and training.

•••• **www.runningnetwork.com**
An excellent review of running shoes.

•••• **www.runningtips.com**
Some good basic running tips.

•••• **runningshoes.com/hp.php3**
Prices on some major brands of running shoes.

•••• **www.cybernude.com/nuderuns**
Calendar of nude running events. I thought I'd throw this in just to keep you inspired.

This was called jogging when we were younger but now it's running even though we've slowed down to what could be called jogging at best. It wouldn't seem you'd need lots of information to just run but that's the kind of world we live in now. Special shoes, special shorts, magazines, coaches and heart monitors just to mention a few.

Weight Lifting

After 50 the tone in your upper body starts to deteriorate. Well actually it started to deteriorate after you stopped playing football in high school but it becomes much more noticeable after 50. The most efficient way to exercise the hundreds of muscles in your body, short of doing manual labor as your main job, is by lifting weights. Learn something about it here.

members.xoom.com/duranman

A good introduction to strength training and bodybuilding.

ftp.cray.com/pub/misc.fitness/ misc.fitness.faq.html

A fabulous site that answers questions and gives advice on every conceivable kind of exercise. If you have to look at one site on fitness make it this one.

www.worldguide.com/Fitness/stex.html

More strength training exercises, with instructions and photos, than you could do in a month of Sundays.

www.lastingresults.com

This site offers very concise and sound advice and a very practical list of 10 weight exercises.

www.frsa.com/fgallry.html

This is an inspirational site, to encourage you, by showing the kinds of women you are likely to see when you join a gym.

Motorcycles

•••• www.motorcycle.com

The world's largest motorcycle online magazine.

•••• www.harley-davidson.com/harley-davidson.asp

The Harley-Davidson home page.

•••• www.museum.sturgis-rally.com

The National Motorcycle Museum with a few good pictures.

•••• www.accessoryinternational.com/directoryapparel.htm

Motorcycle apparel so you can look the part.

•••• www.clarity.net/~adam/buying-bike.html

An excellent used motorcycle buying guide in the event you're getting serious about this thing.

•••• www.motorcycle.com/mo/mcmuseum

A very interesting online motorcycle museum.

It seems like every 50 year old I know is looking for a Harley these days. I figure they're reliving some Marlon Brando fantasy and when they realize how heavy and hard to handle a Harley can be, they'll give it all up. But if you can't live out your fantasies at 50 when are you going to.

Car Racing

Car Racing has come to mean going to a track and taking lessons, not speeding to your beach place waiting for the radar detector to go off. These schools are authentic but expensive. More sensible, of course is to let someone else risk their body and you just watch the race on TV.

www.nascar.com

The official Nascar site with schedules standings and news.

espn.go.com/auto

Covers Formula One, Nascar, Indy, CART, NHRA with schedules, standings and results.

www.na-motorsports.com

North American Motorsports. All kinds of racing and rally and hill climbs, race driving schools, news and discussions.

www.scca.org/index.html

The Sport Car Club of America lets you in on club racing and rallies. You don't get speeding tickets here, you get trophies.

www.racesearch.com

When you want to speed up your old sedan to pull away from the state troopers this is the site that can outfit you.

www.usatoday.com/sports/motor/autos.htm

USA Today coverage of all phases of racing and schedules.

Boxing

www2.xtdl.com/~brasslet

Internet boxing records archive. Biographies and records of all active boxers and all time greats. Truly everything about the fighters.

www.sportingnews.com/boxing

Boxing news and previews from this online magazine.

www.cyberboxingzone.com

This is a fun site for online boxing news with all sorts of historical information as well as streaming video and sound clips. A good rainy afternoon's entertainment.

www.ipcress.com/writer/boxing.html

Boxing on the web brings you rules, rankings, news and statistics.

www.boxingranks.com

Honest Howie's boxing ratings, predictions and latest boxing news.

A great spectator sport that has become even more available with cable TV. Invite friends over and smoke cigars, drink and gamble. It'll make you feel good.

Scuba Diving

Scuba diving and snorkeling are great sports for 50 year olds. They are relatively stress free on your muscle and bone structure and health wise all you have to worry about is being eaten by sharks, having your ear drums blown out by pressure and drowning a black horrible death. Fortunately these things don't happen too often and thankfully, not so far, on any of my dives.

www.scubacentral.com

A good general site that has a tremendous amount of information including equipment reviews, learning to dive, places to dive, chat, and great photographs.

www.mtsinai.org/pulmonary/books/scuba/contents.htm

This is a very comprehensive book that explains all aspects of scuba diving.

www.scubadiving.com/gear

Rodale's Scuba Diving Magazine site with excellent reviews of equipment and dive spots along with articles on photography and all aspects of the sport.

www.padi.com

Padi, one of the main certification services, maintains this site with information on all of their courses and details on diving travel.

www.3routes.com/scuba/index.html

This site tries to list every dive resort and live aboard in the world. They list over 4,000 and have reviews of many.

Other Sports

•••: **www.campnetamerica.com**

A great source of everything you need to know about camping and campsites in case you absolutely insist on sleeping in the woods rather than a motel.

•••: **www.hunting.com**

Information on hunting licenses and equipment, apparel, footwear etc. Be careful not to shoot the campers.

•••: **www.geocities.com/Colosseum/Sideline/5762**

This extensive directory lists more martial arts than you ever dreamed existed and it takes a brave 50 year old to start at this stage of your life.

•••: **www.bowl.com**

Championships, news, links, coaching and everything else you can think of about bowling.

•••: **www.swiminfo.com**

The latest race results, workouts and techniques, a good buyers guides, swim camps, all time records, and probably cures for athletes foot.

•••: **skicentral.com**

A ski site that seems to have everything including almost 6,000 snowsport sites equipment, racing daily ski guides and even a web cam at the top of Mt. Washington.

We must have lots of leisure time in the modern world because there are an incredible profusion of sports to both do and watch not to mention hobbies and vacations. The internet alone could probably suck up most of the rest of your life and you couldn't even get through the "A's".

Cars, Clothes, and Homes

Every 50 year old is a purchasing agent making daily decisions on what to buy and how much to spend. I can't begin to cover all your buying decision needs but have listed a few fun things and a few major ones in this section. Some general advice? When buying a car never be hesitant to walk out; and when buying intimate apparel do it in a neighborhood where they won't recognize you.

Real Estate

www.domania.com

If you're buying, selling or just looking this site provides all the tools and information of prices, values , taxes etc. It has an enormous archive of home sales.

realestate.yahoo.com

You can search the real estate market nationwide for a home based on your criteria and compare cities based on things like cost, crime and income.

www.realtor.com

With over 1 million listings this site lets you find a neighborhood, Realtor and lender. They will even estimate your monthly mortgage payments.

www.ziprealty.com

They claim to be the first online real estate brokers and will give you access to loans, home inspection, insurance and, oh yes, homes.

www.owners.com

You can list your own home for $99 to $289 and avoid paying 6% to a broker.

www.forsalebyowner.com

Another sale by owner service which offers various deals for listing your house.

If you own your own home and even if you don't have the slightest thought of moving check out some of these real estate sites and get a value on the place. It'll make you feel real good. If you're renting I'd just skip on to something else.

Men's Clothing and Fashion

Remember Nehru Jackets? How about wide ties or skinny ones for that matter? Don't be caught in out-of-date clothes. Ask the kids, you're probably hopelessly dressed as it is. These sites might help but I doubt it. Us 50 year olds don't take kindly to change.

www.dailynewsrecord.com

The Daily News Record is the men's fashion magazine and while it is meant for the trade if you are serious about keeping up with trends this will help you. Otherwise you'll be bored to death.

www.firstview.com/mendesignerlist/Gucci.html

Runway fashions from Gucci, no less. Most 50 year olds would have to be pretty brave to wear this stuff.

www.costumegallery.com/men.htm

The history of menswear this century. See if any of the outfits you're still wearing are historical (or hysterical).

www.landsend.com

A super mail order company that has a fine range of casual clothes, dress shirts and accessories.

www.brooksbrothers.com

Check out Brooks Brothers and at least you'll know what you should be wearing.

Tools

•••• **www.garrettwade.com**
Really beautiful woodworking tools.

•••• **www.toolsforless.com**
They claim bargain prices on brand name power tools.

•••• **www.woodcraft.com/woodcraft/homepage.asp**
An online catalog of woodworking tools.

•••• **www.toolbazaar.co.uk/tools_sale.htm**
A really neat site in England selling antique tools.

•••• **www.housemart.com/refer1.asp**
With 35,000 tools you can spend all Sunday afternoon here.

•••• **www.northwestpowertools.com**
You'll find everything here from generators to jointers.

•••• **www.northerntool.com**
This catalog has hand and power tools but also a superb collection of generators, motors, garden equipment, and home construction stuff.

Most guys love buying tools and hanging out in hardware stores. We may never use the stuff we buy but it's nice to have them "just in case". Here is a bunch of tool catalogs that you can peruse on your computer. It's fun to have a package or two arrive every now and then with more tools, and then you can buy more gadgets to hang them up with.

Car Buying Information

The consumer has become empowered, when buying a car, with all the information available on the internet. Not only can you find dealer's cost (sort of; they're getting cleverer) but you can also get quotes from a wide range of dealers.

www.autosite.com

A great site with dealer invoice prices, used car values, photos, specs and everything else to help you buy a car.

www.aautomall.com

Automall searches over 600 dealers and lets you email them for quotes on the car you want. It also has information on warranties, insurance and everything else involved with buying a car.

www.carprice.com

Car, truck and motorcycle pricing guide and information on negotiating, recalls, insurance, leasing, rebates and all.

www.caranddriver.com

Car and Driver magazine's online site with excellent car reviews and articles. Check out their 10 best cars of the year.

www.autobytel.com

Invoice prices, safety records and car reviews make it easy for you to buy a car.

Car buying information

www.dealernet.com

There are almost 7,000 dealers represented here. Check out free quotes from one near your home.

www.consumerreports.org

You have to subscribe but Consumers Reports supplies excellent ratings and recommendations on nearly 200 models. You can also subscribe for their price reports giving dealer's costs.

www.nhtsa.dot.gov

Your government provides lots of information on the safety of vehicles and other life saving concerns. It is worth checking out before selecting a car.

www.kbb.com

The famous Kelly Blue Book gives you the used car values that the dealers laugh at and you can never get when you try to sell it yourself.

www.carorder.com

You can pick the options you want and actually buy the car at this site.

The car industry seems to be moving in the direction of buying cars directly from the manufacturer and even having them build these cars to order. My guess is that this will lead to some really awful color schemes.

Car Repairing

You can't have the old buggy repaired on the net but you can get enough free advice to do it yourself or at least talk intelligently with the Service Manager for all the good that'll do you.

www.cskauto.com

Maintenance tips plus a place to buy all the parts you break trying to fix the parts that are broken.

library.thinkquest.org/19199

Great online courses on how your car works. These courses range from those for novices to professional repairmen.

www.autosite.com/garage/garmenu.asp

With this repair encyclopedia and troubleshooting guide even your wife will be able to fix cars.

www.allexperts.com/browse.asp?Meta=12

An incredibly valuable site where you can submit questions on car repair and get an email response from experts.

www.haynes.com

This is the place to buy your Haynes Manual with detailed repair information on almost any car.

www.autorepairconsultant.net

A free general question consulting service that will answer your questions by email. They charge $25 for specific printed material and training.

Intimate Apparel

www.victoriassecret.com
The women in Victoria's Secret catalog are truly world class.

www.imt.net/~lingerie/index.html
Custom tailored intimates.

www.lingerie-store.com
The descriptions are in French as well as English so it must be sexy.

www.lingeriemart.com
They claim to be the largest source for all kinds of wholesale lingerie and from the size of their site I can believe it.

www.shoptheplaza.com/playstor/4ever.html
A large selection of sexy and erotic lingerie.

www.lusciouswear.com
Very sexy fine lingerie.

emporium.net/avalon
"Drift to a place where romance and innocence meet."

www.business.mcmaster.ca/courses/s727/davio/bridal.htm
Bridal peignoir sets, lace chiffon charmeuse gowns, baby doll sets and such.

It's always fun to look at lovely women in their underwear which is really the purpose of this page. As a public service to 50 year olds I am providing these sources which are also great fun to surf even if you don't need a gift. But, you can also pretend it's for Valentines Day or a special someone's birthday and you need a romantic gift.

Intimate Apparel

I was having so much fun researching these sites that I thought you too would enjoy a few more. I for one don't remember figures like these before "breast enhancement" became fashionable.

•••⦂ **www.azzuma.com**
Pamper yourself in luxurious French lingerie.

•••⦂ **www.fredericks.com**
Frederick's of Hollywood site.

•••⦂ **www.oohlala-kirkland.com**
Catalog of bustiers, body suits, camisoles, sleepwear, teddies, chemises, and more in regular and plus sizes.

•••⦂ **www.firoza.com/peignoirs.html**
A classy collection of designer peignoirs and intimate apparel.

•••⦂ **www.silknchoices.com**
Silk and lace bras, panties and everything else.

Bathroom Remodeling

- **www.kitchen-bath.com/bbasics.htm**

  Bathroom design basics in case you are seriously interested in a remodeling job. Check out the "toiletarium" section if you feel like most guys about this part of the bathroom.

- **www.us.amstd.com/scripts**

  If you want to view some luxury bathrooms the American Standard site is a nice place to start your dreaming.

- **www.hometime.com/projects/ktchbath.htm**

  All the how-to information if you are planning a remolding bathroom job. Don't forget the saunas, spas and steam rooms.

- **www.nkba.org**

  The National Kitchen and Bath Assoc. gives you worthwhile tips on remodeling as well as links to manufacturers.

- **www.bathweb.com**

  A complete directory to the bathroom industry. You can find every thing here including group bathtubs.

If you are like me you spend happy hours in your bathroom either contemplating weighty matters, reading, wallowing in a tub or even doing your necessary business. There is no sense spending all this time in uncomfortable surroundings and these sites will show you just what kind of luxury is possible. It's a good place to spend money since all real estate brokers say it increases the value of your home.

Financial and Legal

You're 50. It's time to think about finances and retirement and to start managing your resources more seriously. These sites can open up a vast exciting world of money management. Just don't rush to quit your job and become a day trader.

Employment

- **www.suite101.com/welcome.cfm/
  50_issues_and_employment**

  Here you'll find real scary articles on finding jobs
  after age 50. I wouldn't read them at all unless you
  own your own company. A superb site, however, for
  employment after 50.

- **content.careers.msn.com/gh.cfm**

  Good hints on resumés, interviews and negotiating
  offers. You'll feel so confident reading this you just
  might quit your present job.

- **midcareer.monster.com**

  A monster employment site that lists hundreds of
  thousands of jobs. Somebody out there must be
  looking for you.

- **www.careermosaic.com**

  You can post a resumé here or search under
  whatever criteria you wish.

- **www.careerweb.com**

  Good career guidance, that I fervently hope you
  don't need, plus the usual resumé and job
  searches.

Your working
position is probably
secure as all get out
and these sites are
included only to
show you how easy
it is to get a job
nowadays so you'll
feel even more
secure. Should you
really be looking
you will find a
whole new world of
job hunting. If you
have specialized
skills or just general
experience, and by
the time you're 50
you have to have
experience, it's
likely someone is
looking for you.
With the internet's
help it's become
easy to find these
companies.

Social Security Information

Remember all those deductions from your paycheck? I thought so. Well, some of those payroll taxes start coming back in about 15 years. Make sure some computer glitch didn't mess up your records.

www.ssa.gov

This government site is a little overpowering with all its information but is a good place to start checking to be sure they have records of all your money.

www.ssa.gov/about.htm

All the Social Security Administrations literature on retirement and things. It's fun to start planning.

www.ssa.gov/mystatement

Request a statement and check if those guys in Washington have had their greedy fingers in your account.

www.ssas.com

The Social Security Advisory Service provides non-governmental help to claimants, provides links and answers questions.

www.cpsr.org/cpsr/privacy/ssn/ssn.faq.html

Answers to interesting questions about Social Security.

Stocks and Investments

moneycentral.msn.com/investor/research/welcome.asp

Money Central's stock research tool with lots of information on just about every company that's traded.

www.nyse.com

New York Stock Exchange quotes, listings and links to the listed companies.

www.nasdaq.com

All the information for stocks, indexes and companies listed on the NASDAQ.

dowjones.wsj.com/p/main.html

The Dow Jones index, its products and services.

www.cnbc.com

Business information, stock reports, a ticker search engine and financial data.

www.cnnfn.com

CNN financial news.

At the time of writing this book everybody and their brother was day trading and investing and making a fortune and the number of sites trying to take a share of this money was mind boggling. Who knows if it can continue but if it does it seems only fair that 50 year olds should play a little and take their share of the pot. It's better than spending your money gambling, but then again maybe it's the same thing.

Stocks and Investments

With the vast amount of financial information on the internet every 50 year old dodo can have the tools to make intelligent investment decisions provided he makes the effort to study and understand. Remember, you are competing against professionals who spend all day analyzing this information, not just a few hours on the weekend, and who have in addition a network of buddies providing inside intelligence.

•••❖ **www.etrade.com**

Get in on the next Microsoft, Intel or Cisco and leave millions to your college for a new athletic center.

•••❖ **www.smartmoney.com**

All the same market information all over again. There must be money here someplace because there sure are a lot of sites.

•••❖ **www.mfea.com**

The mutual fund investor's center with lots of information on mutual funds and 100 definitions that you'd better learn before you start to seek your fortune.

•••❖ **www.hoovers.com/ipo/0,1334,23,00.html**

IPO Central. Get in on a "sure thing" with Initial Public Offerings

•••❖ **www.bigcharts.com**

Charts of all the companies plus interactive charts to help you make your investment decisions.

Financial

•••• **www.cfol.com**

This is the world's largest business and financial search engine.

•••• **www.financialweb.com**

If you can absorb as much financial information as this site offers you must be in the investment business already.

•••• **www.expertstocktrader.com**

They promise fast execution of your trades at low prices.

•••• **www.bay-street.com**

Financial resources for the individual investor.

•••• **www.fool.com/radio/radio.htm**

The Motley Fool takes an unconventional approach to investing and going against the conventional thinking is often the smartest way to invest. I like this site.

The vast amount of data on the internet is enough to make me happy to turn the whole thing over to my broker. If you do invest on your own, one good bet would be to specialize in a few small companies where it is possible for you to become the expert. Good luck and please don't call me with sure fire tips.

Mutual Funds

These sites will give you a good overlook of mutual fund, their performance, who is running them, their focus and fees. Leave your investment decisions to 27 year old kids who have never seen a down market and probably sniff cocaine.

•••• www.standardandpoors.com/onfunds

Standard & Poor's Select Funds is an exclusive designation that indicates a fund has passed rigorous standards for continuity of performance and management.

•••• www.fundalarm.com

This free site rings the alarm when managers change or funds change ownership. It's good stuff to know.

•••• www.fundsinteractive.com

The web's top rated fund site with every thing from fund basics to news to profiles of managers. Links to 120 mutual fund groups.

•••• www.fundz.com

The top 10 load and non load funds, all the major ratings of funds performance, research, top 40 fund internet sites and such.

•••• members.aol.com/plweiss1/mfunds.htm

Mutual Funds Made Simple. Practical guidance on investing money, terminology, questions and answers and other information for beginning and intermediate investors.

Law

••••◦ **www.vix.com/pub/men/harass/harass.html**

Sexual harassment law in case you're not being careful at work.

••••◦ **www.lawyers.com/lawyers-com/content/hiring.html**

Good tips on hiring a lawyer and even advice on what it will cost.

••••◦ **www.abanet.org/referral/home.html**

If you need a lawyer the American Bar Assoc. will give you the names of a few million.

••••◦ **freeadvice.com**

This site offers answers to about 3,000 legal questions but if you have a good personal injury case they'll probably be at your door before you can turn your computer off.

••••◦ **www.lawyers.com/lawyers-com/executable/ask**

Some very good answers to legal questions. At least one good lawyer dedicated his or her time to this site.

If you have ever been involved in a legal dispute you know how expensive lawyers can be. It is very often even more expensive to think you are a lawyer and try to do it yourself. Actually you can't win and that is why everyone feels the way they do about lawyers and there are so many "lawyer" jokes.

Law

Practicing law by yourself can be dangerous but running to your lawyer for every decision will bankrupt you. The best approach is to have one of your kids go to law school and advise you for free.

www.law.cornell.edu

If you are really ready to be your own lawyer this site gives you good pointers with constitutions, codes, court opinions and even ethics.

www.divorcenet.com

While I hope you will never need it, this site gives you a state by state breakdown of divorce law with lots of information on fathers' and even grandfathers' rights and everything else.

www.legaldocs.com

Write your own wills and leases. Save money and only get into trouble later. (just kidding). Some forms are free and others from $3.50 to $27.75.

www.lawresearch.com

The Internet Law Library. This is the real McCoy and you can reference from 20,000 to 200,000 resource links should you happen to have time this afternoon.

www.catalaw.com

The catalog of catalogs of worldwide law on the internet. From aboriginal to women and gender law.

Veteran's Affairs

••• **www.va.gov**

Check on the benefits and services you're entitled to and don't let the burial and memorial stuff make you nervous. You made it this far didn't you?

••• **www.vnis.com**

A Veteran News and Information Service. This will surely bring back some memories.

••• **www.military-network.com/MainSite.htm**

Locate lost buddies, find out about reunions and a ton of other military information most of which you were happy to forget.

••• **www.militaryusa.com/vietnam_vets_data.html**

Extensive list of reunions, 2.7 million name database of Vietnam Veterans plus lots of help in locating anyone else who has been in the military.

••• **www.bravo.org/features.htm**

A neat site that offers service to all veterans and helps with things like buddy search, reunions and outreach services.

Nowadays kids don't know about military service. But we do, whether it was the best or worst years of our lives. These sites will help you find old army buddies and to check on any benefits that might be due you.

Food and Drink

By the time you're 50 you probably have established some strong preferences in what you eat and drink and have become a bit of an expert in your favorite wines or beer or Chinese food. Even so, you're going to love getting more information on delicious things to put in your stomach and if these sites cause your eating and drinking to get a little out of hand you can always drop back to the Health and Fitness section and check on the latest diets.

Cooking

•••: **www.agrotrade.com**

A fascinating place to shop for spices from around the world as well as tea, dried fruit and candies.

•••: **www.cornwellcoffee.com**

Fresh Kona coffee direct from Hawaii. It sounds delicious.

•••: **www.cooking.com**

The master site for cooking with lots of cooking gear for sale as well as recipes, products and techniques.

•••: **food.homearts.com/food**

A recipe and restaurant finder as well as lots of tips and suggestions all of which are going to kill your diet.

•••: **www.foodsubs.com**

The Cook's Thesaurus with substitutions for thousands of ingredients. You can, for example, substitute Gow Choy for Ku Chai or Garlic Chives. Now I never knew that.

Expand your horizons with these sites and discover new taste temptations and new restaurants. Then gain weight and go on another diet. It's the cycle of modern man

Cooking

The greatest chefs have traditionally been men so don't be afraid to play in the kitchen. Men are more daring and imaginative and can come up with great dishes that will impress their woman and friends. Women are much better at cleaning up afterwards and it's wise to leave those tasks to them.

www.epicurious.com

Thousands of recipes, kitchen equipment, basic skills and even the etiquette on eating an artichoke, among other things.

www.geocities.com/NapaValley/4079/index.html

The list of almost 20 online cooking magazines alone will keep you busy for the rest of your life. The history and legends of foods is fascinating and then there are the recipes.

www.escoffier.com

This is a site for professional chefs but it has a great section telling you how to become one.

www.inquisitivecook.com

A super data base of answers to questions about cooking.

www.hoptechno.com/book1.htm

Dietary guidelines for Americans and splendid tips for healthy food preparation.

Some Fun Foods

•••• **4bagels.4anything.com**

What is a bagel and what is its history. This site has this kind of interesting information along with shops and franchises should you want to go into the business.

•••• **www.gourmetgarlicgardens.com**

How to grow garlic, its health benefits, all the varieties and probably vastly more than you'd ever want to know about garlic.

•••• **www.matkurja.com/slo/country/food/gobe**

How to find and prepare wild mushrooms without dying, which seems a goodly thing to learn.

•••• **www.dzpickles.com**

Make your own pickles and sauerkraut with the kits this company sells.

•••• **www.fritolay.com/pretzel.html**

The history and story of the pretzel.

The garlic and pickles will make you burp, the mushrooms may kill you but nutritionists figure that bagels and pretzels are health foods so I've covered all the bases on this page. Have fun learning more about these fun foods.

Beer

When we started drinking beer the taste was pretty much limited to the mild lagers that still make up the bulk of what's sold here. But recent years have spawned thousands of micro breweries with intriguing tastes and varieties that make choosing a beer a wonderful adventure. It's worth experimenting. If nothing more, your refrigerator will look more colorful.

www.breworld.com

Europe's large and excellent internet site for beer and brewing. Superb beer industry search engine plus hours of fun exploring breweries and ranking beers.

www.800-microbrew.com/

For $29.95 each month you get 3 beers from 4 different microbreweries. The site also has a newsletter and recipes.

www.aardvark.ie/beamish/

Visit Beamish, in Cork Ireland, brewing genuine Irish Stout for over 200 years. It's a fun tour.

BeerMasters.com/BeerMasters

Beer Masters Tasting Society provide a superb glossary to help describe what you drink. Acetaldehyde, for example, is a green apple aroma produced as a by-product of brewing. You really don't need to know that to enjoy a beer.

www.siebel-institute.com/welcome

A school that teaches you to brew rather than just drink, like when you went to college.

Beer

••••• **www.beerhunter.com**
A splendid online magazine by Michael Jackson, the world's foremost beer journalist.

••••• **www.Heineken.nl**
A history and a virtual tour of the Heineken brewery.

••••• **www.guinness.ie**
The history of Guinness and lots of other fun information.

••••• **www.fostersbeer.com**
You have to enter your birth date to see this site (hey, we're 50) but they do teach you to speak Australian.

••••• **www.pubcrawler.com/Template**
A great site listing almost 4,000 micro breweries, more than you could sample in a lifetime, plus reviews and beer talk.

Don't let "experts" dictate what beer you should like and don't let descriptions of beer become as outlandish as those given to wines. Beer, after all still makes a 50 year old burp and pee.

Dining Out Restaurant Guide

There are so many restaurants out there that it is comforting to have a few guides to help you pick out the good ones. It's too bad they don't give you information on the available lighting. I'm having a little trouble reading menus in dark places.

www.zagat.com

Zagat is the world's best restaurant review guide. It uses reader's ratings to rank the restaurants and I have seldom known it to be wrong. Unfortunately it covers only major cities.

www.food.com

Takeout or delivery from thousands of restaurants near your home.

www.restaurants.com

A list of restaurants in cities across the country and maps to help you find each.

www.fodors.com/ri.cgi

Fodor's expert restaurant reviews for restaurants in the cities they cover. You won't find every one listed but they tend to find the better places.

www.dinesite.com

Restaurants listed by location and broken down by cuisine and type. The ratings seem to be very generous.

www.restaurantrow.com

Would you believe 100,000 restaurants listed in 24 countries. You could starve to death just deciding which to visit.

www.menusonline.com

A great restaurant guide for 16 major cities with menus, reviews, directions and even dress codes.

ine

•••⋮ **www.wine.com**

They have an enormous inventory of wines and prices to choose from and then they somehow get it to your door. A little educational material also.

•••⋮ **wineserver.ucdavis.edu/Acnoble/waw.html**

For $6 you can buy a plastic wine wheel which helps you communicate about wine by using analytical terms rather than vague ones. Oaky, buttery, black peppery, it's all beyond my nose.

•••⋮ **www.winespectator.com**

The online version of Wine Spectator magazine. The wine basics are excellent for the unknowledgeable and will really teach you about wine.

•••⋮ **hwww.drinkwine.com**

This site has all sorts of information for the wine lover from food pairings to wine tours to growing your own.

•••⋮ **www.vine2wine.com**

A comprehensive wine site that connects you to everything. Sites like these could put authors like me out of business. In practice, however, even these good ones disappear.

At 50 some of us have graduated from the screw top caps and straw Chianti bottles that we used to stick candles in at college. Some may even have become wine snobs with different glasses for each variety of grape and a descriptive vocabulary of tastes that sounds like a botany textbook interspersed with a barrel maker's inventory list. The sites shown here are for us 50 year olds in the middle who enjoy a good bottle of wine and haven't yet started annoying our friends with flowery descriptions.

Wine

I like reading wine reviews but I can never find any of the bottles reviewed when I go to a wine shop. I wonder if everyone has this problem. Don't let price influence your buying decisions. Expensive wines rarely come out on top in blind taste tests.

www.wino.net

All about wine law, investing in wine and wine's health benefits.

www.wineculture.com

A hip wine guide to choosing, storing, buying, serving, and saving what's left.

www.tablewine.com

This site discusses affordable wines, around $10, with different topics each month.

www.wineauthority.com

Very authoritative and insightful wine reviews.

www.bandc.com

Reading this informative wine education site of over 200 pages will leave you sober enough to drive home.

www.stratsplace.com/wine.shtml

A superb site with thousands of the usual but also neat stuff like uses for corks, removing wine stains and printing wine tasting sheets.

Wine

www.thewinenews.com

This wine magazine reviews over a hundred wines each month and I particularly like the double blind tastings.

clifty.com/wine

A great wine tasting site run by regular folks like you and me and, in fact, here is a place where you can post your own ratings.

www.wineenthusiastmag.com

The Wine Enthusiast magazine, rating and selling everything that has to do with wine.

www.veronafiere.it/slowines

A wonderful Italian site which rates wines from around the world.

www.homearts.com/helpers/winenav/wine1.htm

The Wine Navigator has a good wine glossary and information on choosing wine and matching it to food.

Pick up a few terms from these wine sites and you can probably match wits with your friends who are wine experts. When giving gifts of wine I find it's usually safest to give bottles that my more knowledgeable friends have given me.

Wine and Beer Making

I think every 50 year old tries this at least once. I did. The beer wasn't too good but was fun to make but then like most things you get interested in, something else comes along and now you have a bunch of bottles and stuff at the bottom of a closet.

•••• www.telusplanet.net/public/bhuisman/winetips.html

Good advice for learning to make your own wine.

•••• www.hwbta.org

The Home Wine and Beer Trade Assoc. will teach you the basics and put you in touch with retailers who can sell you the equipment.

•••• www.leeners.com

This well designed retailer's site shows you all the ingredients and equipment for making all kinds of booze as well as vinegar, cheese, mustard and soap. Hey, you can be self sufficient and go live in the woods.

•••• www.beerbrew.com

Another fun site that will sell you all the equipment you need to try beer and wine making as well as providing instructions.

•••• members.iquest.net/~ericg/ferment.html

This site tells you how to make simple fermented drinks and doesn't even try to sell you something. Sites like this are getting rare these days.

Scotch

•••• **www.scotch.com**

This distiller gives the history of the drink along with recipes and bulletin board.

•••• **www.whiskyweb.com**

If you love scotch whiskey you've found your site. The latest news and tastings and the renowned Malt Whiskey File.

•••• **www.scotchwhisky.com**

The complete guide to scotch whiskey. How it is made, the complexity of its taste and all the different kinds of blends and singles.

•••• **www.scotchdoc.com**

"The Scotch Doc" provides great information about the whiskey and, among a lot of other information, leads a 20 minute tour showing how it is made.

•••• **www.dcs.ed.ac.uk/home/jhb/whisky**

A wonderful non-commercial site that gives histories and descriptions on all Scotland's distilleries.

•••• **www.maltwhisky.org/default3.htm**

A wonderful site with lovely pictures and the tasting notes of the author.

Maybe you have to age a bit like a fine bottle of scotch to fully appreciate the drink. When younger we may have indulged in the clear liquors but with maturity something like a single malt intrigues us.

Bourbon Whiskey

Bourbon is the most famous of the 4 American Whiskeys. It got its name from a town honoring the French Royal Dynasty for help during the Revolutionary War. Bourbon is distilled from at least 51% corn which is responsible for its sweet taste. Most come from Kentucky and Tennessee.

www.thewhiskystore.com/beginner/bourbon.htm
This site tells you about bourbon and has pictures of such interesting bottles that you just want to rush out and buy some.

www.straightbourbon.com
History, makers, brands and tasting notes on this very nicely designed site.

www.kybourbon.com
The Kentucky Distillers Assoc. will tell you what makes their bourbon special and the history of the product.

www.bourbon-whiskey.com
Tasting notes, distillers, cocktails and news and you won't understand a word since it's all in Japanese. Good fun.

www.jackdaniels.com
Jack Daniels, home site of the oldest distillery in the country, with a nice tour of the facilities.

Drink Recipes

•••:• **www.bardrinks.com**

Welcome to the party place. Drinks are categorized in many ways so you can find just the one you're looking for.

•••:• **www.angelfire.com/mo/bartrick/bartrick.html**

This is a fun site with bar tricks played with napkins, matches, glasses and things found around a bar. It also has drinking games, toasts, aphrodisiacs, recipes and more.

•••:• **www.idrink.com**

Just enter the ingredients you have around the house and this site will tell you what cocktails you can make. It sounds like there is a good party game here.

•••:• **www.drinkboy.com**

A nice alphabetic list of recipes for every drink you've ever heard of plus articles and discussion of bar tools.

•••:• **www.inforamp.net/~mcdermot/drinks.html**

An extensive list of readers' submissions of recipes. They range from "A Nother One Of Those" to "Zombie Piss".

> Having a cabinet full of colorful and weirdly shaped bottles and a collection of mixing tools is almost as much fun as coming up with the concoctions. We used to call this our chemistry set.

Cigars

Cigars aren't quite as hot an item as they were a few years ago but guys our age enjoyed cigars long before they became a fad. One disadvantage of having cigars become a fad has been the prices. Popular and rare smokes have shot through the roof. On the other hand there's a lot more ratings and information and brands available and that does making smoking cigars more fun. There's no indoor place left, of course, where you can smoke them.

www.cigars.com

There are over 100 links here with every conceivable kind of information about cigars. Humidors, discount cigars, vintage cigars, and lots of cigar companies.

www.cigargroup.com

The Internet Cigar Group is an excellent site with some real solid information on all aspects of cigars. Their cigar brand database is very extensive.

www.cigaraficionado.com

This online version of Cigar Aficionado Magazine keeps you up-to-date with everything happening in the cigar world. Ratings of nearly 1,300 cigars.

www.cigarlife.com

An internet cigar magazine with daily news, monthly columns and feature articles. Their top 10 cigars each month is a fun section.

www.cigarfriendly.com

Cigar friendly restaurants throughout the country as well as cigar reviews and events.

Hobbies, Pastimes and Interests

Hobbies may sound a little juvenile for a 50 year old but we all have these little collections and interests and I guess they qualify as hobbies for lack of a better word. And when dignified with the title "hobby" there is much less chance your wife will want to put the collection in the garage to make more space for her own doodads which also could be called hobbies but we usually refer to as "junk collection".

Model Railroad

My parents always told me I was "too old for trains" so I never got any. I've always wanted a set and just might buy myself some for my next birthday.

www.mcs.net/~weyand/nmra

The site of the National Model Railroad Association which has served the needs of model railroaders since 1935. Lots of links to anything you'll need.

rr-vs.informatik.uni-ulm.de/rr

This interactive site lets you operate a model railroad on your screen. That way you don't have to worry about the dog running off with the caboose.

www.caboosehobbies.com

They claim to be the world's largest train store and with 150,000 items they just might be. Links to train historical societies and manufacturers.

207.5.46.132/tm.htm

An index of what seems like every model train magazine from 1934 to the present.

www.trainweb.com/modelrailroad

Enough links to keep you "hobbied" out for the rest of your life. Everything from building your own steam engine to contacts with loads of model train clubs.

www.highiron.com

Classified ads, well organized so you can buy or sell almost anything in the model train field.

Photography

•••• **www.photography.com**

A pleasant site with a good "Ask the Pro" section, photo news, search provisions and a daily contest.

•••• **www.onlinephotography.com**

This site has some gorgeous photos and a well done, if limited, product review section.

•••• **www.kodak.com/US/en/nav/takingPics.shtml**

Kodak's classic Guide To Better Pictures. This advice is so sound and so basic it makes you wonder why 95% of the photo-taking public ignores it. Worth reading and rereading.

•••• **www.bath.ac.uk/~masres/photo/manual.html**

A good basic introduction to photography. Email this to your friends who are not good photographers and looking at their pictures will be much less painful.

•••• **home.netcom.com/~nikonman/phototips1.html**

Very sound tips from a pro. This site is eminently readable and full of good ideas.

Everybody is a photographer and if everybody would just look at a few of these sites and learn how to really use their cameras we'd all be a lot less bored looking at everybody's boring pictures.

Gardening

This is a well covered subject on the internet and there are innumerable sites. I've just listed a few to help you get started but just type in "Gardening" and you'll be still reading while your garden withers away from lack of attention.

www.garden.org

The National Gardening Association has articles, tips and answers to your questions.

www.garden.com

A good place to buy 20,000 different products for your garden. Beautiful photos.

www.gardenguides.com

Wonderful garden guides to everything you may want to plant plus lists of mostly free catalogs.

www.gardenweb.com

Lots of gardening resources are listed here with links to specialties such as Kitchen Gardens and Wildflowers. There are sections on seed exchanges and a botany glossary.

www.gardenweb.com/vl

This site is a true web of gardening information and as you scroll down you will find everything you're looking for.

www.coronaclipper.com/ornam_trees.htm

Pruning ornamental trees hedges and shrubs.

treeselect.com/treesearch.htm

Here is a great data base of trees categorized by color, shape size, growth rate and everything else you can think of.

Flying

•••• **www.avhome.com/clubs-org.html**

This site has a long list of flying and soaring clubs and of flying organizations. If you're new to flying, contacting a local club is a good way to start.

•••• **www.landings.com**

A very comprehensive site with every weather link known, flight planning, pilot supplies, aircraft sales and hanger talk just to name a few.

•••• **www.faa.gov**

Once again your government offers an excellent site with all sorts of FAA information. Regulations, pilot requirements, safety issues and so much more that only a government agency has the wherewithal to delve into.

•••• **www.homebuilt.org**

There's no need to take up flying and spend a fortune buying an aircraft. With this site you can choose from dozens of designs and easily build your own plane. No thanks. I think I'll take the bus.

•••• **www.aeroseek.com/links/Images**

Links to wonderful collections of fascinating aircraft pictures. This will fire you up to get a pilot's license.

•••• **www.aeroseek.com/links/Training_and_Education**

This is the site that will teach you how to fly. Links to loads of schools and courses.

> I've always wanted to fly and own a plane but every time I read about a private plane crash I get the willies. Do you think 50 is too old to learn to fly a helicopter? That's my real dream.

Model Making

Model cars and model trains and steam engines or whatever. All the things that are too big or too impractical to own in full size make up the appeal of creating them in miniature. That plus the ability to keep a collection of the little objects without filling your garage or hanger or local railroad yard.

www.modelspot.com

This English company is a specialist in model making and browsing its site will make you feel like a kid again.

looksmart.remarq.com/looksmart/category.asp?p=sports+%26+recreation%3Amodels

This is one long address to type in correctly but it is the internet discussion network where you can share ideas and get advice and is perfect for model makers. Find launch areas for your rockets or helicopter fuel for your creations.

members.aol.com/CHRISBOSCO

If your hobby is making miniature helicopters or aircraft this site has everything you'll need.

www.4milmodels.com

Four mil miniatures of all kinds of military figures and equipment.

www.dscshowcases.co.uk

Glass showcases for all the things you make that will keep your wife, kids or cleaning people from breaking them.

www.arrakis.es/~mny/directory0.html

Everything on model ship building and collecting. Many, many links to clubs and sources worldwide.

Coin Collecting

••• www.coinlink.com

You have just about everything here: auctions, books, coin grading, dealers and mints.

••• www.coinsite.com

A spectacular image gallery of rare coins plus answers to all your numismatic questions.

••• www.cybercoins.net

This online coin dealer has prices, descriptions and illustrations of expensive coins that they sell along with news and articles.

••• www.limunltd.com/numismatica

A great site with information about all phases of numismatic interests. News, frequently asked questions and a long list of splendid articles.

••• www.rare-coins.net

This site lists prices they'll pay for coins and currency. It's too bad the design is in gold on black cause you can barely read it.

This is one hobby where you should make money if you don't do something stupid and buy just at the top of the market like my friend Ed did when gold reached $800. Rare coins have historically increased in value and they're small enough to hide in an old shoe.

Billiards

You've got to admire guys who can really move those balls around a table. I'm so bad that the only time I pick up a cue is when there is no one around to see.

www.billiardinfoline.com

Places to play, tournaments, equipment, instruction and news.

www.sound.net/~jimbarr/docs/websearch

An extensive directory to help you find pool halls, cue makers, instruction, books, leagues and whatever amongst 1,000 pages of billiard things.

www.billiardworld.com

Billiard World Magazine covers the rules of pool, tips, pool personalities and various forms of pool artwork.

www.poolrooms.com

The best poolrooms in America. A colorful site that lets you search by a map and gives a description of each pool hall.

www.billiardsdigest.com

Online magazine that gives tournaments, news, and talk.

www.interplay.com/games/vrpool.html

They claim this virtual pool simulation will teach you to play the real game. Don't believe it.

Stamp Collecting

••• **www.philatelic.com**

An online mall for stamp collectors with many dealers, classifieds, bulletin board and library.

••• **www.usps.gov**

The U.S. Post Office site with the latest stamps and stamp collectibles. It's good business for them. The profit's enormous when selling a stamp that doesn't get used.

••• **www.philately.com/philately/index.htm**

This site has a database, among much other information, of every country that ever issued a stamp and it's very long with some places I guarantee you've never heard of.

••• **www.stamplink.com**

This site claims to be the best in its category and it certainly seems to have links to the entire world of stamp collecting. I wouldn't start here unless it was a very rainy Sunday.

••• **www.linns.com**

This is the largest weekly stamp newspaper and besides keeping up-to-date you can search for zillions of stamps.

••• **alfin.computerworks.net/index.html**

A good beginner's introduction to stamp collecting and an easy site from which to get started.

> The hobby of kings and presidents and anyone who may have to flee a country at a minute's notice and would like to take some of his ill gotten gains with him. Just kidding. I'm sure most of my readers are honest hobbyists.

115

C ar Collecting

Now here is a hobby that will eat you out of space as well as money. I've tried it and car collecting is very expensive. Be smart and just visit museums and look at all the lavishly illustrated books and internet sites. Maybe the smart thing to do is combine this interest with model making and collect only miniature cars.

www.classicar.com

Just about everything from classifieds to chat to event calendars.

www.archive.vintageweb.net

A thousand great photos of vintage cars and motorcycles.

www.traderonline.com/coll

If you are seriously looking they have over 50,000 cars for sale plus lots of information.

www.myclassiccar.com

Information and good browsing and evidently the whole Hemming's catalog of cars for sale.

www.antiquecar.com

Antique and classic cars for sale with great pictures.

www.classictruckshop.com

In the event you really have room in your driveway you can also collect classic trucks.

Astronomy

•••• **www.scopereviews.com**

A great site about telescopes and superb advice for beginners.

•••• **www2.astronomy.com/astro**

Astronomy Magazine's online site. I have always found that magazines about a hobby or sport is a good place to start when exploring a new interest. Read them first before running out and buying the equipment.

•••• **www.seds.org/galaxy**

Some truly exciting pictures and a good guide to the solar system and space sciences.

•••• **www.mtwilson.edu/Services/StarMap**

This site creates a free map of the sky customized for your locations and viewing time.

•••• **galaxy.tradewave.com/galaxy/Science/Astronomy.html**

This site indexes everything from extraterrestrial life to planetariums.

•••• **www.solarviews.com/eng**

Magnificent views of the solar system. If this doesn't get you interested in astronomy nothing will.

•••• **www.seds.org/images**

Space Images Archive with 13,000 breathtaking photos.

Think of how impressed everyone will be when you can name a constellation other than the Big Dipper. It also gets you out of the house if you're a cigar smoker.

Family

Up there with your health, your family is the most important part of your life so you might as well expand your knowledge of relationships with the help of the internet. Likely your kids are teenagers who will disappear from the human race until it's time to go to college at which time they'll reappear asking for even more money. There is no hope understanding women so I haven't even bothered to list sites dealing with that subject, but I have included your best friend, the dog.

Fatherhood

•••• **www.fathermag.com**

Fathering magazine has many articles on problems of custody and single parenting and a wonderful list of articles under "The Joy Of Fathering" section.

•••• **www.vix.com/pub/men/nofather/nodad.html**

A library of articles on fatherhood and fatherlessness.

•••• **www.peak.org/~jedwards/paternity.html**

Paternity information page. "Everything fathers need to know and what the government fails to tell you."

•••• **www.cyfc.umn.edu/Fathernet**

FatherNet produces information on the importance of fatherhood, fathering and shows how fathers can be a good parent.

•••• **www.fatherhoodproject.org**

This educational project develops ways to support men's involvement in child rearing. Lots of good links and reviews of books and videos.

In the old days the father just had to "bring home the bacon" and maybe do a little disciplining and toss a ball around on weekends. But things have changed and now you'll have to read books and check out these sites to teach you the whole child raising business.

nteracting With Your Kids - Theme Parks

They may no longer want to play sports with you and are mortified over what you say when you drive them with their friends and are embarrassed by what you wear and think all your ideas are weird, but if you invite them to a theme park they will be your best pal again. Here are a few.

www.screamscape.com

A theme park fan's personal guide and best touring tips to parks and attractions. Great reviews of rides.

members.aol.com/parklinks/links.htm

Absolutely total coverage of the entire theme park, carnival , state-county fairs, fun centers and ride world. They even have accident reports so you can work up your excuses for rides you'd rather skip.

www.geocities.com/~robbalvey

A couple's guide and ratings of theme parks and roller coasters. And, if you can stand it, 300 photos of their roller coaster honeymoon.

users.sgi.net/~rollocst/amuse.html

Links to every amusement, theme, water park and every other kind of fun center you can imagine.

themeparks.about.com/travel/themeparks

You can find every theme park, roller coaster, zoo and whatever in the world with this site.

Slang and Language

•••⦂ **www.slanguage.com**

American Slanguage guide that lets you pick a city and talk like the locals or look up the latest teen talk. Dat is crunk.

•••⦂ **www.peevish.co.uk/slang**

This site lets you plug in a word and find out its meaning. It's from the United Kingdom, where so much slang originated, so they should know.

•••⦂ **www.miskatonic.org/slang.html**

This claims to be a glossary of hardboiled slang but you'll actually recognize some of the terms. It's a long list and you'll enjoy becoming hip as you face this new language.

•••⦂ **www.csupomona.edu/~jasanders/slang**

College slang. You'll love the top 20 list. It has every word your kids use and you don't.

•••⦂ **www.rapdict.org**

This is a serious list of rap slang but I suspect it is out of date by the time it arrives on the internet.

•••⦂ **dir.yahoo.com/Reference/Dictionaries/Slang**

This site lists a load of slang dictionaries and if you get into them too deeply your own family will no longer understand you.

Are you having trouble understanding your kids? Do they use terms like peeps and warsh and yo sup that you have no idea of the meanings? The sites listed here will make you hip again so you can say all these cool things and sound like an idiot teenager whenever you want. Also, don't forget to put your hat on backwards.

Grandfathering

Maybe you were lucky. Perhaps you married as a teenager and your kids did the same and now you're a young grandfather. They tell me it's one of life's greatest experiences. While I ain't one yet I can dream and at least imagine what sites will be valuable for a grandfather. Perhaps the first thing you will need to learn is current trends in toys. What more can a grandfather do than bring a toy.

www.drtoy.com/drtoy

Dr. Toy rates toys and lists the top 100 toys and has links to places you can buy them.

www.etoys.com

This site certainly makes buying toys easy with an age directory and recommended favorites.

imageplaza.com/parenting

Great advice on raising children. You'll wish you read this before raising your kids. Now you can advise your children on how to raise your grandchildren. They'll just love you for it.

iml.umkc.edu/casww/grandparentsraising.htm

Here is a site on grandparents raising their grandchildren and I hope the only time you need this is when you're baby sitting.

www.grandparenting.org/Research.htm

A long list of articles on grandparenting. You will find something here that applies to you.

Colleges For Your Kids

www.review.com

This site of the Princeton Review has everything you'll need to know about getting into any college. They even have a separate place for parents to click on.

moneycentral.msn.com/family/home.asp

Tips on saving for college, selecting a college and paying for college. What else do you need to know?

www.embark.com

Find, apply to and get your kids into the right school. You can search out any college and apply to leading colleges online.

www.usnews.com/usnews/edu/college/corank.htm

The U.S. News and World Report's annual college rankings. Find out if your old school still makes the grade.

www.universities.com

A data base of 3,000 colleges and universities broken down in many ways and with financial aid information.

www.collegeview.com

Virtual tours of hundreds of colleges. It sure beats driving all over the countryside.

No, it's probably too late for you to sign up to get your MBA. The college sites I'm listing are so you can stay knowledgeable about schools for your kids. They're not going to listen to you but if you beat them to the punch and have some ideas on schools and courses, with luck, you can nudge them in the right direction.

Kids Camps and Trips

50 year olds should go on exotic or active or just relaxing vacations. In order to do this, you are going to have to find a great trip or camp for your children. The sites listed here will give you ideas for hundreds of exciting places to send kids which will educate them, broaden their horizons, expand their interests and leave you guilt free to take your own vacation.

www.camp.ca

Just type in the kind of camp you think your offspring would be interested in whether it's sailing, riding, computer, cheerleading, gymnastics, foreign or weight loss and so many names will come up that you'll never be able to interview them all. It's unbelievable but there is a camp for every interest.

www.kidscamps.com

Another directory of camps that offer so many choices your kids will be fighting to go.

www.summercamp.org

This free public service will give you guidance and referrals for camps worldwide.

www.outwardbound.com

Teenagers should get excited about these adventure trips. In fact I got pretty excited and they take parents on some.

www.nols.edu

National Outdoor Leadership School offers superb leadership and outdoor skill courses in exciting wilderness areas.

Dogs

www.petnet.com.au/selectapet/dogselectapet.html
Select a dog that matches you and your life style at this site.

www.petnet.com.au/dogs/dogbreedindex.html
Photos and descriptions of most every breed to let you see if you're going to like the dog the computer picked for you.

www.bulldog.org/dogs
Doggy information on the web. Links to specific breeds and all sorts of other information. My God they even cover wolves.

dogs.about.com/pets/dogs
Everything you need to know to care for your dog: grooming, health, housebreaking, food, training, shows plus lots more.

www.petrix.com/dogint
This site ranks the intelligence and obedience of various breeds. Don't feel inadequate if your pet comes out in the lowest quarter.

www.akc.org
Lots of help from the American Kennel Club on selecting and buying a pure bred dog.

There should be someone in the family that you can really count on and if you take care of the feeding, your dog is going to be the one. He may protect the house and play with the kids and go to the vet with your wife but if you feed old Fido you are the one who'll get licked each night when you come home.

Good Stuff For Guys To Know

If wives, kids, or women friends ask questions, us guys, more so since we're 50, have to know all about whatever they are asking especially if it has to do with something mechanical. These sites will give you enough information so you can bluff your way out of almost any question.

www.howstuffworks.com

The How Stuff Works site will make you seem like a genius. It tells you how everything works and your kids and woman will think you're absolutely wonderful.

www.britannica.com

The whole Encyclopedia Britannica. What more could you ask for as an information source. I wonder what ever happened to all those people who used to sell them door to door?

www.wackyuses.com

You'll impress everyone when you show them how Coca Cola® can clean a toilet bowl, you can shave with peanut butter, use Jello® to style your hair and Miracle Whip® to remove chewing gum or dead skin.

www.virtualflowers.com

Send virtual flowers, for free, to your wife, mom or girlfriend. They'll love it. I've been meaning to send them to my wife for months.

www.urbanlegends.com/index.html

Hundreds of all those crazy stories you've been hearing all your life like alligators living in sewers and cow tipping and Spanish Fly are investigated, and discussed and mostly debunked here.

aps

••• www.mapquest.com

Not only maps of every place but a detailed visitor's guide for everything you'll need from hotels to theaters once you get there.

••• www.maps.com

If you need to buy folding maps this site has plenty for sale as well as an atlas that pinpoints what's available for any country.

••• www.maps.expedia.com/OverView.asp

A great site that lays out a map giving you accurate directions between any two points in North America. See how it gets you home.

••• www.mapblast.com/mblast/index.mb

Free maps and driving directions to all points in the U.S.

••• geog.gmu.edu/projects/maps/cartogrefs.html

This cartography resource has links to almost 100 internet map sites.

••• oddens.geog.uu.nl/index.html

This site has links to almost 10,000 map resources. If you can't find it here you probably don't want to go there.

All guys love maps because if we have maps then we don't have to ask directions. And no guy likes to ask directions.

Women don't understand that asking directions is an admission of weakness that we would prefer to avoid. After all, the male species is the hunter and provider who can make his way through trackless wastes and dark jungles to feed his family if only he has a map and compass.

Maps

There are lots of places to get maps online and if you're a "map nut" like I am you can have hours of fun as well as finding your way to a friend's new house.

•••• **www.library.yale.edu/MapColl/online.html**

A neat site showing pictures of Yale University's historical map collection for the period 1500 to 1900.

•••• **hum.amu.edu.pl/~zbzw/glob/glob1.htm**

Several hundred great images of the globe with fantastic space views, maps of surface temperatures, glaciers, fires, winds, everything.

•••• **www.mapsonus.com**

This great site will draw a map of any address you type in or plan you a route between any two points.

•••• **www.nationalgeographic.com/resources/ngo/maps**

National Geographic's site of maps and flags and world information.

•••• **www.nationalatlas.gov**

U.S. Geological Survey shows just how much fun you can have with your tax dollars. Play with maps of all the U.S.

•••• **terraserver.microsoft.com/default.asp**

Amazing as it sounds this site allows you to zoom in from space and see an aerial view of your house.

Good Information Sources

•••:• **www.usps.gov**

The post office site with prices and rates. Find out what that airmail letter to Afghanistan should cost.

•••:• **www.reversephonedirectory.com**

Have a friend's phone number, but need their address? Use the Reverse Phone Directory. Also great if you have Call Identifier and want to know who called you while you were out.

•••:• **www.usps.gov/ncsc/lookups/lookup_zip+4.html**

Need someone's zip code? Just enter the address, and you'll come up with their zip code + 4 as well as their county.

•••:• **www.smartraveler.com**

Traffic updated frequently for major cities in the US, with links to city-related travel services.

•••:• **www.govworks.com**

This site offers a free service finding information or answering questions about any of your governmental needs.

> Besides knowing all about mechanical things you can impress people with knowing how to find zip codes and addresses, weather, traffic and the correct postage to put on a package to Finland. It's all here.

Film and Video Reviews

Why go to lousy films and rent boring videos just cause your wife, kids or friends pick them. Get the real ratings and reviews at these sites and make your own decisions. I for one like pirate movies.

www.filmgeek.com

Very complete reviews of new film and video releases.

www.film.com

In depth reviews of current films, and there are more than you can imagine, plus any video you can think of.

www.imdb.com

A data base of every film released since the beginning of the century. This may be the best movie and video site on the web. They even tell you how to sell your old videos. And best of all, you can find movie theater schedules in your area and what's currently on Pay-Per-View.

mrshowbiz.go.com

Another wonderful entertainment site with TV ratings as well as films and videos.

www.movie-reviews.com

Excellent and easy to use film and video reviews with star ratings.

Film and Video Reviews

•••⦂ **www.filmsite.org**

The Greatest Films specializes in classics.
Wonderful descriptions of their top 100.

•••⦂ **www.reel.com**

Good reviews of current films as well as videos
and DVD's.

•••⦂ **entertainment.msn.com/movies/movies.asp**

Just type in your zip code and it will give you
theaters and showtimes.

•••⦂ **www.foreignfilms.com**

This is the place to find great foreign films on
video and DVD.

•••⦂ **www.cinema-sites.com**

Films and video reviews, data bases, fan pages,
trivia, scripts, schools and so much more it'll
take you all afternoon just to get through the
index.

It's fun, after
50 years of seeing
films to look at lists
of the best ones
and realize just how
many you've seen
or missed.

The Men's Movement

Since most 50 year olds are confirmed male chauvinists we don't know much about the Men's Movement unless we have been through a child custody battle or sexual harassment suit. The Men's Movement feels we have been persecuted for years and it's time to unite and receive some justice from those women libbers who have made our life hell.

www.vix.com/men

This site covers the several men's movements in great detail.

www.widesky.org

Men's movement group fashioned after the "mythopoetic" realm of Robert Bly, the acknowledged founder of the "Men's Movement".

www.vix.com/pub/men/orgs/orgs.html

Lists of men's movement organizations throughout the U.S., Canada and the world.

www.vix.com/pub/men

The Virtual Library provides endless links on men's movement issues.

members.tripod.com/~Alexander_Artist/ home.html

The Men's Rights Movement is a new civil rights movement whose goal is more equality and more rights.

Politics

••• www.e-thepeople.com

No need to go to rallies and risk freezing or even being beaten by the authorities like in the 60's. With this site you can pick an issue right on line and enter your petition.

••• www.politicaljunkie.com

Everything political is on this site. Perspectives, facts and figures, people and organizations, newspapers, government, everything.

••• www.thenewrepublic.com

Washington insider news and thoughtful articles on politics and foreign affairs.

••• politics.slate.msn.com/politics

Top stories and politics from around the country.

••• www.politics1.com

Links to all the political parties, issues and debates. Links to all political news sources, state races and campaign consultants.

••• www.democracynet.org

A public interest site for election information. The site is nonpartisan and funded by foundations.

You better start paying attention to politics if only to make sure there'll be some cash left in Social Security when you retire and make sure those liberals don't tax you out of your birthright.

133

Weather

Remember how old people were always worrying about the weather? When people move to Florida they still delight in telling you just how cold it was last night in New England or where ever else you live. The advent of "wind chill" thrills anyone who lives in a warm climate and has relatives in the cold and a telephone with which to reach them.

www.accuweather.com/weatherf/index_corp
It's fun to enlarge and animate the map.

www.weather24.com
Weather24 will send the forecast to your email address so you'll always have the latest info.

www.cnn.com/WEATHER
If you want the weather in Japanese or Portugese you can get that also.

www.intellicast.com
Weather and forecasts anyplace in the world.

iwin.nws.noaa.gov/iwin/graphicsversion/ rbigmain.html
The most complete, statistic laden, boring and hard to understand site, courtesy of your National Weather Service.

www.weather.com
Just fill in the zip code and up comes the weather. World weather as well and moving satellite pictures.

weather.yahoo.com/index.html
Current weather and 4 day forecasts. Weather maps, worldwide weather, ski reports etc.

www.ncdc.noaa.gov/extremes.html
U.S. weather extremes and global historical records like 523

www.washingtonpost.com/wp-srv/weather/historical/historical.htm
Historical weather for over 2,000 cities. Record highs, lows, rain, clouds, snow and everything else you can think of.

Men's Magazines

•••❖ **www.maximonline.com**

Maxim has beer, travel, fitness and lots of girls and this site gives you a wonderful flavor of the magazine. It's really supposed to appeal to younger guys but if you don't tell anyone you can enjoy it too.

•••❖ **www.gq.com**

This is the homesite of Condé Nast's magazine GQ which once was more fashion oriented and now seems to be leaning more to the sexy stuff to better compete with Maxim.

•••❖ **www.manhood.com.au**

An excellent online Australian magazine with lots of manhood forums and advice.

•••❖ **ww.uploaded.com**

The online version of the very sexy British magazine Loaded. Don't enter here if you are offended by coarseness.

•••❖ **www.askmen.com**

An online men's magazine with a wide range of subjects like women, love, bodybuilding and whatever. It's free.

Men's magazines have been around almost as long as printing. We're not old enough to remember the Police Gazette but I think it showed an occasional picture of some shapely young lady in her underwear and was a big hit in the barber shops of its day. Present day men's magazines show a lot more, of course, but there are also magazines on health and sports and other things. Parts of some are online for free and these lists may introduce you to a few you never heard about.

Men's Magazines

For all their attempts to introduce health, fashion, activities, philosophy and other subjects, most of the general men's magazines fall quickly back to sex. Mind you, I'm not complaining and I do love looking at the pictures.

www.mensjournal.com

A general interest men's magazine with emphasis on adventure, travel, fitness and sport.

www.playboy.com/magazine/current/english

Here is Playboy, the old classic, and you'd better hope your internet access can download photographs quickly.

www.manslife.com/texttoc.html

The complete contents of a man's life and what a lot of information that is. A very informative and extensive magazine.

www.klinks.com/totalman

Total Man seemed like a magazine without direction but the "Babes Of The Day" are fun.

www.everyman.org/index.html

A bimonthly journal of men's issues and interests.

www.ungroomd.com/articles

Some funny articles. It makes you wonder though as to how all these free magazines manage to stay in business.

penthouse.com

You don't have to actually subscribe and be embarrassed when the post person delivers each issue. Most of Penthouse is right here on the web.

Mustaches and Beards

•••• **planet.ten.net/~nbc**

The November Beard Club which encourages the growing of beards, mostly in November. Funny stuff.

•••• **members.aol.com/Beardguy/links.htm**

Good links to beard related sites. I am beginning to think bearded guys are a very interesting group.

•••• **www.zap.org/fuzface/index.htm**

I guess about a thousand photos of guys with notable fuzz on their faces.

•••• **www.best.com/~bigerbtr/beards**

Beards, beards, and more beards.

•••• **www.ragadio.com/oafh**

Organization For the Advancement of Facial Hair. Even more fun.

•••• **www.funfolly.com/h/w/wigchr4.htm**

Some inexpensive, fun beards and mustaches.

Fake Beards

•••• **www.magicmakers.com/retail/beards /beardsmustaches.html**

You can buy any kind of beard or mustache you can imagine and test people's reaction before wasting time growing them.

> At least there is one area in which very few women choose to compete with our sex. These sites mostly glorify growing great beards and mustaches.

Music For 50 Year Olds

You've probably learned by now that "your" music isn't "their" music. Young people laugh at your taste in music but they are probably already too deaf to realize how great it is. Listed here are some places you can find just what you like.

www.oldiesmusic.com

On this site you can search oldies music of the 50's, 60's, and 70's. This is the good stuff that you can dance to, sing to and fall in love with.

www.geocities.com/SunsetStrip/Alley/4795/links.htm

Over 100 links to find The Beatles, ABBA, Simon and Garfunkle, The Rolling Stones and everyone else.

www.on-air.com

An internet-only radio station where you can hear all your old favorites.

www.srv.net/~roxtar/oldies.html

Reviews of songs and artists from your formative years. You'll enjoy seeing the old names.

www.allmusic.com

An incredibly comprehensive source of music information. Thousands of reviews and audio samples, and you can search for anything in 6 languages.

Art

•••⦂ **www.artchive.com**

An archive of over 2,000 works of art from over 200 artists with commentaries and galleries. The scans are excellent and you don't have to worry about crowds at your local museum.

•••⦂ **www.wwar.com**

A worldwide art resource that allows you to search galleries, artists, museums etc. There are for example 945 museums in the U.S. alone which should keep you busy for a few weekends.

•••⦂ **www.artresources.com**

Articles, reviews and guides to shows, museums and galleries plus over 2,000 images in their catalog.

•••⦂ **www.art.com**

Extensive art and poster collection searchable by artist, subject or color.

•••⦂ **www.artcyclopedia.com**

Browse by name or other searches to find any artist. Their top 30 artists, based on web popularity, is fascinating.

•••⦂ **www.artlex.com**

A visual arts dictionary of art-related terms that will allow you to hold your own at a cocktail party made up entirely of art historians.

Did you think this whole book was just going to be fun, beer and intimate apparel and no culture at all? Well here is a section on art and it's going to broaden your cultural coefficient.

139

Find Your Old Buddies

There are lots of people finding facilities on the internet and it's a hoot to look up old friends. Find that bully from the sixth grade or your old high school flame.

www.infospace.com

Just type in the last and first name and, by God, they usually come up. You can also search public records to find out if they still owe you money.

www.theultimates.com

This site searches by several engines and if you use it a lot will give more features and better service for 12 bucks a year.

www.knowx.com/free/peoplefinder.htm

This ultimate people finder uses real estate and change of address records as well as phone books to find the long lost ones.

www.worldemail.com

A world email directory with 18 million listings in 6 different languages.

www.reunion.com

An online missing persons bulletin board and registry. Maybe someone out there is looking for you.

www.search-shark.com

A serious people searcher that uses military records, Social Security numbers, death notices and public records as well as the usual.

G enealogy

•••⁝ **www.cyndislist.com**

The most spectacular genealogy site on the web. Your one stop spot for more than 63,000 links most of which are categorized and cross-referenced in over 120 categories, such as country or religion. Constantly updated.

•••⁝ **www.familysearch.org/sg/DisTree.html**

Site of the LDS (The Church of Jesus Christ of Latter-Day Saints) the foremost source of genealogical records. An excellent way to begin your search with information on methods, addresses of sources, and untold helpful hints.

> Find out if there are any nobles among your ancestors and if there is a castle or crown waiting for you in Slobania.

•••⁝ **www.ancestry.com/search/main.htm**

Constantly updated database of over 500 million names. The information is only available to those who join at a fee, but, if you're intent on tracing your family, this is the place to go.

•••⁝ **www.oz.net/~markhow/ukbegin.htm**

Beginning genealogic research for England and Wales. Links to civil registrations, census returns, parish registers, books and other internet links.

•••⁝ **www.jewishgen.org**

Primary internet source connecting researchers of Jewish genealogy worldwide. Contains a database of over 175,000 surnames and towns, Shtetl links for over 200 communities, and a variety of databases.

•••⁝ **www.polishroots.com/genpoland/index.htm**

If your family came from Poland, this is an excellent place to begin research into your family's history.

•••⁝ **www.geocities.com/SiliconValley/Haven/ 1538/germ_rus.html**

List of German-Russian Genealogy Links.

•••⁝ **www.irish-insight.com/a2z-genealogy**

Over three hundred links to genealogy of Ireland and Northern Ireland.

index

index

OTHER GREAT BOOKS BY BOSTON AMERICA

The fine cultivated stores carrying our books really get ticked if you buy direct from the publisher so, if you can, please patronize your local store and let them make a buck. If, however, the fools don't carry a particular title, you can order them from us for $8 postpaid (unless otherwise noted). Credit cards accepted for orders of 3 or more books.

#2700 Rules For Sex On Your Wedding Night
All the rules from undressing the bride to ensuring the groom will respect her in the morning.

#2704 What Every Woman Can Learn From Her Cat You'll learn that an unmade bed is fluffier and there's no problem that can't be helped by a nap among many others.

#2706 Is There Sex After 50?
Everything from swapping for two-25-year olds to finding out it's not sexy tucking your T-shirt into your underpants.

#2707 Beer Is Better Than Women Because...
Beers don't change their minds once you take off their tops and don't expect an hour of foreplay.

#2708 You Know You're Over 30 When...
You start wearing underwear almost all of the time and no longer have to lie on your resume.

#2709 You Know You're Over 40 When...
You feel like the morning after and you can swear you haven't been anywhere and you start to look forward to dull evenings at home.

#2710 You Know You're Over 50 When...
Your arms aren't long enough to hold your reading material and you sit down to put on your underwear.

#2713 Unspeakable Farts
These are the ones that were only whispered about in locker rooms like the "Hold Your Breath Fart" and "The Morning Fart".

#2714 101 Great Drinking Games
A remarkable collection of fun and creative drinking games including all the old favorites and many new ones you can barely imagine.

#2715 How To Have Sex On Your Birthday
Finding a partner, the birthday orgasm, birthday sex games and much more.

#2717 Women Over 40 Are Better Because...
They are smart enough to hire someone to do the cleaning and men at the office actually solicit their advice.

#2718 Women Over 50 Are Better Because...
They don't fall to pieces if you see them without their makeup and are no longer very concerned about being "with it".

#2719 Is There Sex After 40?
Great cartoons analyzing this important subject from sexy cardigans to the bulge that used to be in his trousers.

#2721 Cucumbers Are Better Than Men Because...
They won't make a pass at your friends, don't care if you shave your legs and stay hard for a week.

#2722 Better An Old Fart Than A Young Shithead
A great comparison of the Old Fart who dresses for comfort and the Young Shithead who is afraid of looking like a dork.

#2726 Your New Baby
This is a manual that explains everything from unpacking your new baby to handling kids' plumbing and routine servicing.

#2729 Great Bachelor Parties
This book tells it all from finding a cooperative stripper to getting rid of the father-in-law to damage control with the bride to be.

#2730 Rules For Engaged Couples
Rules for living together, meeting the family, learning to share and planning the wedding.

#2731 The Bachelorette Party
Great pre-party and party ideas and suggestions for everything from limos to outfits to strippers to your behavior in bars.

#2732 Brides Guide To Sex And Marriage
Dealing with your husband's family and learning what he does in the bathroom and secrets of sleeping comfortably together.

#2501 Cowards Guide To Body Piercing
Cartoons and explanations of all the good and horrible places you can put holes in yourself.

Specially priced books:

#1500 Fish Tank Video [$15 postpaid] This fish tank video enables you to experience all the joys of beautiful, colorful and graceful tropical fish without having to care for them. You'll find yourself hypnotized by the delicate beauty of these fish. Approximately 1 hour running time.

#3001 Winning at Strip Poker [$14 postpaid with playing cards] Not only does this book give you tips on winning at poker, but it tells you how to talk beautiful women into playing with you and shows you what they should look like in 96 pages of full color. It also provides a deck of cards with extra aces to help you win.

#3002 Slightly Kinky Sex Games [$10 postpaid] The games include lots of ideas for oils and ice and places and tie ups and should keep a couple's sex life sizzling with imaginative new activities for a year. 96 pages of sexy full color pictures.

#3003 America's Greatest Hooters [$10 postpaid] 96 pages of full color photographs of America's best including the Louisiana Lollipops, New York Knockers, Georgia Peaches, Pennsylvania Pendulums, Minnesota Minis and lots of others.

NEW INTERNET BOOKS!

#2733 Bizarre Internet Sites [$8 postpaid]
Hundreds of unusual and wild internet sites that will shock, disgust and amuse you and take you places you never imagined even existed.

#3100 Kavet's Internet Sites for Your Wedding and Honeymoon [$10 postpaid]
This is a manual that explains everything from unpacking your new baby to handling kids' plumbing and routine servicing.

#3101 Kavet's Internet Sites for Men Over 50 [$10 postpaid] Fifty year olds need all the help they can get and this book gives them almost 1,000 internet sites.

#3102 Kavet's Internet Sites for Women Over 50 [$10 postpaid] This is a manual that explains everything from unpacking your new baby to handling kids' plumbing and routine servicing.

#3104 Kavet's Internet Sites for 40 Year Olds [$10 postpaid] When you are 40 you are busy with a job and kids and houses and cars. This book gives you almost 1,000 internet sites on these and subjects you'd like to make time for like travel, hobbies and sports.

BOSTON AMERICA C★O★R★P

125 Walnut Street, Watertown, MA 02472
tel: (617) 923.1111 • fax: (617) 923.8839